THE
BUDGET
KIT

Second Edition

The Common Cent$ Money Management Workbook

Judy Lawrence

Dearborn
Financial Publishing, Inc.®

This publication is designed to provide accurate and authoritative information in regard to the subject matter covered. It is sold with the understanding that the publisher is not engaged in rendering legal, accounting or other professional service. If legal advice or other expert assistance is required, the services of a competent professional person should be sought.

Acquisitions Editor: Christine E. Litavsky
Managing Editor: Jack Kiburz
Interior Design: Lucy Jenkins
Cover Design: S. Laird Jenkins Corporation

© 1993, 1997 by Judy Lawrence

Published by Dearborn Financial Publishing, Inc.®

Printed in the United States of America

97 98 99 10 9 8 7 6 5 4 3

Library of Congress Cataloging-in-Publication Data

Lawrence, Judy.
    The budget kit : the common cent$ money management
workbook / Judy Lawrence. — 2nd ed.
        p.   cm.
    Includes bibliographical references and index.
    ISBN 0-7931-2343-7 (paper)
    1. Finance, Personal.   2. Home economics.   I. Title.
HG179.L338   1997
640'.42—dc20   96-36019
                                                   CIP

Dearborn books are available at special quantity discounts to use as premiums and sales promotions, or for use in corporate training programs. For more information, please call the Special Sales Manager at 800-621-9621, ext. 4384, or write to Dearborn Financial Publishing, Inc., 155 N. Wacker Drive, Chicago, IL 60606-1719.

Dedication

To my parents who inspired my skills and interest in managing money through their everyday examples and to Dwight Myers (posthumously) and Carol Myers for their years of dedication to the publishing industry and being instrumental in introducing me to this world.

Other Books by the Author

COMMON CENT$: The Complete Money Management Workbook (Forerunner to the current Budget Kit)

The Family Memory Book: Highlights of Our Times Together

The Money Tracker: A Quick and Easy Way to Keep Tabs on Your Spending

The Budget Kit Multimedia CD-ROM for Microsoft Windows

*A*cknowledgments

My special thanks goes to the following people who helped with the development of this new and revised *The Budget Kit: The Common Cent$ Money Management Workbook,* and to those who gave their support and encouragement during the earlier times as this book metamorphosized through its *Common Cent$* years into the workbook you now hold:

- Kathy Welton, my original editor, for finding me once again and believing in possibilities

- Chris E. Litavsky, my editor for this new workbook, for encouraging me through the wonderful new arrangement and ideas in this workbook and for her incredible skills and gracious professionalism

- Terry Savage, for her continual enthusiastic written and verbal support throughout the years

- Carol Park and Susan Bross for being my professional colleagues and for sharing their ideas, encouragement, and inspiration with me.

- Janie Bluestein, Maya Sutton, and SJ Sanchez for always sharing their love and wisdom and giving their time, assistance, and encouragement when they were needed the most

- Bonnie, Elsa, Bea, and Cynthia for sharing their personal stories with me and sensitizing me to the needs of the divorced parent

- David Levin and Jan Gilman for sharing their legal expertise and guiding me through the legal maze of the needs of the divorced parent

- Especially Glen, Judith, Diane "Kiel Buddy," James, Paula, Kimberly, Colette, Debbie, and the many readers who have used this workbook year after year and have shared their ideas and suggestions, which have been implemented in this new edition.

Contents

*P*reface

We've all heard the saying, "If it's not broke, don't fix it." That idea has certainly applied to this workbook, which has been around since 1981 when it was originally published as *Common Cent$*. Over the years, there have been minor revisions and additions, yet the core worksheets and concepts have stayed the same.

Each revision, including this one, came as a result of many wonderful reader comments and suggestions, as well as my own seminar and one-on-one counseling experience with hundreds of clients over the years. I continue to welcome your suggestions and comments for enhancing this workbook so it fits your needs and helps you reach your goals.

My intention was and still is to provide a guideline or roadmap to get you started that is flexible enough to accommodate the many unique regional and personal situations that exist. The variety of worksheets throughout this workbook are designed to give you an overall view of your monthly and yearly finances at a glance. Modify them if needed to fit your particular needs.

One woman looking at this workbook at one of my seminars asked, "Where's the theory?" The "theory" can be found in almost every personal finance book on the market. I'll bet you have a few of those books on your bookshelves right now. Most of these books discuss volumes of valuable financial information. The authors usually encourage readers to establish a budget or spending plan and briefly discuss and show some examples. That still leaves the actual "doing it" part up to you, and that's usually where the procrastination, confusion, or fear sets in.

If you haven't been taught how to manage money and set up a budget, how would you know what to do? Just having money does not necessarily guarantee your ability to manage it. Not everyone has the time, knowledge, or organizational skills to set up a simple, functional system for managing all their daily, monthly, and yearly finances. That's why I designed and wrote this down-to-earth realistic workbook. Instead of theory, the *focus of this workbook is to complement the other financial books and give you a tool you can pick up, quickly read, and easily and confidently start to use at any time by just gathering your financial papers, pencil, calculator, and eraser.*

As a counselor, I originally designed this workbook for young families and for women who were suddenly widowed or divorced, had limited money management skills and often were intimidated by the whole idea of dealing with money. I have since realized, through my seminars and from the many letters and phone calls I have received from people of all professions and incomes, that managing finances is a universal concern.

What I have also seen become a major universal concern over the years is consumer debt. We've all seen the effects of the spending in the '80s and how it is now affecting our debt in the nineties. Now, more than ever, the Debt Payoff Record section of this workbook will motivate you as you see at a glance your progress toward financial control and ultimate financial independence as you pay off your debt.

Once you take the time to start organizing and planning your financial affairs with these worksheets, the results will be extremely rewarding. Remember, this workbook is a tool for you to use. By itself, it will not change anything. With your input and your consistent and thorough participation in setting your goals, planning your expenses, recording and paying attention to your spending, and utilizing the many valuable sections, this workbook will help you create magic with your finances.

The magic will be in the form of financial peace of mind replacing financial chaos. Bill paying will be manageable. Getting into the savings habit will be easier and more rewarding as you use the different savings records and watch your balances grow. Tax time will go more smoothly when you use the tax-deductions record. Keeping child support records will also be easier with the special worksheet.

And finally, life will take on a whole new meaning when your stress is reduced and you can focus on other aspects of your life besides money.

It is extremely gratifying to hear from so many of you since *Common Cent$* was originally published and to learn how this workbook helped you buy your first home, save your marriage, finally get out of debt, and start saving and investing money for the first time.

Using this workbook, as many readers have told me, can literally change your life. I look forward to hearing how it changes yours. I wish you a successful and prosperous year.

How to Use The Budget Kit

This workbook took some of the fear out of money for me. By setting up an amount I knew we could spend in an area, I didn't feel so bad when I was spending that money. I knew it was planned and okay. Before I was always in fear or guilt over everything I spent.

THE PURPOSE OF THIS WORKBOOK

The Budget Kit is designed to be easy to understand and practical to use. Because it is flexible, it can be used immediately regardless of the time of year or the condition of your finances. By following the guidelines in this workbook, you will learn to take charge of your overall finances by anticipating your monthly and yearly expenses, instead of always reacting to crisis after crisis.

There are two purposes for this workbook. The first is to help you get your financial information organized and keep proper records. With this workbook, you can keep records of your daily, monthly and yearly expenses, medical costs, installment payments, credit card charges, mail order purchases, child support payments, savings, investments, retirement and much more.

The second purpose is to help you successfully plan and manage your finances. You can list and plan your goals; work out an estimating method for paying yourself (savings), your bills, and your monthly expenses; remind yourself of items you need or want to buy when extra money is available; and plan ahead for the periodic, but anticipated, expenses throughout the year.

One couple depends on the routine of planning meetings to keep their household of five flowing smoothly. "Every Sunday night when the kids are in
bed, we sit down and talk about the finances. We make decisions about expenses and decide if we should spend money on something or save it."

HOW TO GET STARTED

Set aside a block of time so you can thoroughly review the variety of sections available in this workbook. These sections contain instructions along with worksheets that were designed to address many different needs. Each worksheet can be used independently or with another. Determine your own needs and see how this workbook will best fit them.

The many helpful worksheets in *The Budget Kit* are divided into three parts.

Part One helps you focus on where you are and where you want to be financially. Your *initial* time involved may be greater here as you gather and fill in the information. After completing this step, these pages become more of a place to revisit for reviewing and reflecting as the year goes on.

If this section feels a little overwhelming at this time, or you are very anxious to get started and want to jump right in and set up a spending plan, then move on to Part Two. Take a moment to skim through this section and come back later and complete it when it feels right for you.

Part Two is your action section where you plan, project, and record on a daily, monthly, and yearly basis. The bulk of your time and attention will be spent in Part Two throughout the year. You will quickly see how to anticipate those "unexpected" bills throughout the year, know how to plan out each month in advance, and learn where all your money is going.

Part Three is a collection of a variety of record keeping worksheets for accommodating different individual needs. This is where you can keep records concerning child support income, mail orders, subscriptions, investments, retirement, savings and other miscellaneous information. You can also record your expenses like medical and dental (including insurance reimbursements) as well as tax deductions.

Take some time to look through these three parts and each of these worksheets and see which ones will be more helpful for your particular financial situation.

PREPARE FOR THE KNOWN, THE UNKNOWN, AND YOUR DREAMS

By setting up your system for the year, you are planning ahead and getting a full financial picture. It won't be long before you see that you will need to have some system for saving money ahead of time for different purposes. Listed below are three different areas of savings I recommend you have eventually.

1. Reserve Account (The *Known* Expenses)—After listing your major anticipated periodic or nonmonthly expenses throughout the year on your **Yearly Budget Worksheet** in Part Two (such as car insurance, home improvement plans, tuition, gifts, etc.), total these up.

Divide this total number by 12 to get the monthly amount you need to set aside in a bank, credit union, or money market account for a reserve account. Remember, this is not your emergency money. This is a savings for money that will be due, only at different times of the year.

By setting this money aside each month, you will feel like you magically have extra money available when some of the bigger expenses (like car insurance or graduation) come due. These infrequent expenses no longer will disrupt your whole monthly budget or land on your credit card.

Enter this reserve savings category and amount on your **Monthly Budget Worksheet** in Part Two under "Fixed Amounts" at the top part of the page. Consider this part of paying yourself first as one of the fixed bills you pay each month.

2. Emergency Account (The *Unknown* Expenses)—There are going to be times when unknown disasters occur which create emergencies. Some examples are when the car breaks down, the home heating system needs to be replaced, your job position is eliminated, or your dental bridgework breaks.

The best way to have some peace of mind through any of these events is to know you have funds set aside.

The guideline amount has been to have three to six months' worth of take home pay available. Save this money in a bank, credit union, money market, or mutual fund with check writing privileges.

Determine what amount you can save each month (you may want to use payroll deductions) and slowly build this account up. Enter this amount under "Fixed Amounts" as well on the **Monthly Budget Worksheet** in Part Two.

Again, this money is *not* to be confused with the reserve account, which actually is being held for expenses that have already occurred or will occur.

3. Goals Account (Your *Dream* account)—An entire section in Part I is devoted to identifying goals and saving for them. This is the third amount that will be included under "Fixed Amounts" on the **Monthly Budget Worksheet** in Part Two. Initially this may be a much smaller amount or even nonexistent until the other two accounts get started and have sufficient totals available.

By including your Reserve, Emergency and Goals Accounts on the **Monthly Budget Worksheet,** you have a way of putting together and seeing your total spending plan. This process also reminds and encourages you to save and put funds aside regularly, offering you a system for staying in control of your finances.

WHO MANAGES THE FAMILY BUDGET?

In most households, one spouse or partner assumes the role of "The Family Budget Director" and keeps that role. This can, of course, be logical and efficient provided this person is good at managing money and enjoys doing so. I recommend that each spouse be involved with the household finances and responsibilities at some point even if he or she does so every other year.

By getting involved with the family finances on some regular basis (every six months, or year, or two years) you develop an awareness and understanding of your financial obligations, expenses, limitations, family spending patterns, and overall current financial status.

This awareness is important for personal relationships. If both parties earn money, but occasionally the party managing the finances must announce that certain items or luxuries are not affordable, the news can cause all kinds of bad feelings, confusion and misunderstanding for the uninvolved party. "Why not? We were paid just three days ago. What are you doing with the money?" is not an uncommon response.

Without a total sense of the family finances, it is difficult to know what you really can and cannot afford.

This awareness is especially important if there is ever an extended incapacitating illness, a divorce or a death in the family. When the spouse not familiar with the family finances suddenly is responsible for them, this can be a very overwhelming experience.

TAKE CHARGE OF YOUR LIFE AND MONEY

The methods and guidelines in this workbook will show you how to set your goals, watch your spending and plan your expenses. You then will find that your bills are paid on time, more money is saved than you ever thought possible, your investments are off to a healthy start, your goals are being reached, and the stress in your life is reduced.

As you take charge of your money, you will notice this control carrying over to other aspects of your life. Your relationships with your family will become more relaxed and more time will be available to pay attention to other things in life besides money.

Best of luck as you begin your new money management program!

Part One

Net Worth Statement

Identified Goals Worksheet

Goals Savings Record

Needs/Wants List

One longtime reader wrote to say, "When I started keeping records it was like an awakening. In seven years I saved $100,000 thanks to your book. By the end of this year, which will be just over nine years, that number should be close to a quarter of a million." It's amazing how the numbers start to accelerate after a certain point.

This reader was exceptionally disciplined and motivated. Whenever he did not spend money (i.e., walk versus taxi, video versus movie, library versus bookstore) he would actually put that savings aside and record it in his book. On last conversation he still continues to feel no deprivation. He now *knows* he can buy anything he wants, and is very satisfied with how he chooses to spend his money.

As you fill in the following pages in Part One you will see more clearly what you already have and what you still would like to have.

Writing down what you want in black and white is always a powerful way of becoming more focused and motivated in your daily living. Part II will give you the tools for accomplishing your goals.

Net Worth Statement

An important step in gaining financial control is to take an accounting of what your total financial worth is. Every year, your net worth should be tabulated to enable you to review your progress and compare it with your financial goals. In addition, a Net Worth Statement is a valuable aid in planning your estate and establishing a record for loan and insurance purposes.

Net Worth Statement

Date Completed _____

ASSETS—WHAT YOU OWN

Cash: On Hand _____
Checking Account _____
Savings Accounts _____
Money Markets _____
Other _____

Real Estate/Property:
Home _____
Land _____
Other _____

Investments: (Market Value)
Cash Value Life Insurance _____
Certificates of Deposit _____
Stocks _____
Bonds _____
Mutual Funds _____
Annuities _____
IRAs _____
401(k) or 403(b) Plans _____
Pension Plan/Retirement Plans _____
Other _____

Loans Receivable _____

Personal Property: (Present Value)
Automobiles, Vehicles _____
Recreational Vehicle/Boat _____
Home Furnishings _____
Appliances and Furniture _____
Collectibles _____
Jewelry and Furs _____
Other _____
_____
_____
_____

Total Assets

LIABILITIES—WHAT YOU OWE

Current Debts:
Household _____
Medical _____
Credit Cards _____
Department Store Cards _____
Back Taxes _____
Legal _____
Other _____
_____

Mortgages:
Home _____
Land _____
Other _____

Loans:
Bank/Finance Company _____
Bank/Finance Company _____
Automobiles, Vehicles _____
Recreational Vehicle/Boat _____
Education _____
Life Insurance _____
Personal (from family or friends) _____
Retirement Accounts _____
Other _____
_____
_____
_____

Total Liabilities

Total Assets minus Total Liabilities = **Net Worth** _____

Setting Financial Goals

Jan was never successful at saving even though she made a great income as a loan officer. Once she started tracking her spending and learned how to work out a budget it made a "million percent" difference in her life. She created a savings account to buy a house, which she never could do before. She practiced the "pay yourself first" technique, considered her savings as a bill, and successfully saved $15,000 in one year and bought her house. Now she's even more motivated about savings and is planning to invest in additional real estate.

Setting financial goals is one of the most important steps for gaining financial control. When you have a goal, you have the motivation needed to follow a money-management plan.

The worksheets on the following pages will help you identify and record your financial goals and develop a plan for reaching them.

To begin, ask yourself what is important to you. What will make you happy and/or be a significant accomplishment? Define your goals in specific attainable terms (such as buying a red two-door BMW instead of just a new car) and write them down. You then have taken the first step toward reaching your goals.

IMMEDIATE/SHORT-RANGE GOALS

These goals are any that you have identified for the next month and/or year. Your goals depend on your interests and your lifestyle. Perhaps you want to save your Christmas money in advance this year, buy drapes, or pay off a major debt.

Do not forget your emergency fund. If you do not have at least three months' take-home pay set aside as a protection against unforeseen problems or disasters, this should be your *number-one goal.* Once you have the security of knowing you are covered for possible emergencies, you can comfortably focus on your other goals.

When you reach the goals you have identified in this section, you will have more confidence and discipline for the more aggressive goals in the Middle-Range/Long-Range Goals section.

MIDDLE-RANGE/LONG-RANGE GOALS

Middle-range goals are those you hope to reach two to five years from now. Maybe you are dreaming of a new home, thinking of starting a family or planning a trip abroad.

Long-range goals include plans beyond five years, including college tuition and retirement. By thinking about longer-range periods, you will make wiser use of your money. With time on your side, small amounts of money saved for 10 to 40 years will grow tremendously. And if you pay closer attention to where you invest your money, it will grow even more.

FAMILY AFFAIR

If you have a family, bring everyone together to discuss their interests and goals. Children need to take part in this activity not only to give their input, but to learn from the process for their own adult years.

There seldom is enough money to reach everyone's goals. When Dad wants a boat, Mom wants a piano and

Junior wants a VCR, compromise is necessary. Each member of the family has to give and take and decide what is agreeable as a compromise. Rather than drop a major goal altogether, try delaying the deadline date.

One family decided to cut back and save up for a car. In two-and-a-half-years' time this family of four with two young children saved up $18,000. They did not consider it depriving when they chose to cut back on clothing and eating out and did a lot more buying at garage sales and auctions. Each month they also invested $300 without exception in a mutual fund as a dollar cost average approach. The best part was feeling confident in their ability to actually pull it off.

FILLING IN YOUR IDENTIFIED GOALS WORKSHEET

Once you have defined your goals and have written them down under "Goals," fill in the remainder of the chart. Number the "Priority" of each goal listed. Which goal do you want first, second, etc.? Which can wait a few months or another year?

What is your "Date Needed"? Six months, one year, six years? Every goal should have a beginning and an ending date. Once you have committed yourself to a time frame in your mind and on paper, you have taken one more positive step toward reaching your goal.

"Cost Estimate" helps develop your estimating ability and forces you to do some research. By calling, reading or shopping to determine the estimated cost of buying a computer or putting in a pool, for example, your goal becomes more than just a dream.

If you have money in savings, how much of that "Amount Already Saved" do you want to use toward your goal? Write it down. Commit yourself to an amount.

"How To Achieve" is crucial. What are you willing to do to make your goal a reality? Will it involve working overtime or finding a second job? Will it mean trade-offs—cutting back or eliminating expenses such as movies, meals out, or smoking—so you can reach your goal?

How much will you have to save each week, month, or year to reach your goals? If you have a difficult time setting aside money for your goals, arrange with your bank for direct deposit from your paycheck.

The Goals Savings Record worksheet is a great place for keeping track of your savings for your goals. Take your "Cost Estimate" figure and write it in the space next to "Total Cost." Divide that figure by 12 to see how much money you need to save every month. Each month, record your savings and balance. You will be excited to actually see yourself coming closer to your goal each month.

PAY ATTENTION TO YOUR MONEY

If you have a strong desire to reach your goal and you *really* want your money to work for you, you must pay attention to what you do with your money.

Earlier, I mentioned having time on your side and paying closer attention to your money. For long-range goals (college, early retirement) where large amounts are necessary, these two factors are critical.

Let's say that you decide to save $100 at the beginning of every month for ten years to reach your goal. You could stash that money under your favorite mattress and have $12,000 at the end of ten years. Obviously, that method is not the wisest or safest.

If you had chosen to take that monthly $100 to your bank and let it sit safely in a savings account and draw 3 to 5 percent compounded daily interest, after ten years you would have made nearly $2,000 to $3,500 more "free" dollars for doing nothing more than driving to your local bank. In the meantime, you would have saved $15,536.81 for your goal.

On the other hand, if you were to take time to find an account that gives 10 percent compounded daily interest for that same $100 every month for ten years, your reward for your research time would be an extra $4,995.61 over the 5 percent interest or an extra $8,532.42 over the mattress investment, giving you $20,532.42 for your goal!

Saving $100 a Month for Ten Years		
Under the Mattress	3–5% Interest	10% Interest
Total Saved $12,000	$15,536.81	$20,532.42

These figures do exclude the inflation factor; however, the more years you have to invest and the higher interest rate or return amount you get, the more money you will make. Read financial books and magazines or talk to your local banker, broker, insurance agent, or financial planner to examine your options. *When you learn how to effectively invest your hard-earned money, you can be confident that you will reach your goals.*

IMMEDIATE/SHORT-RANGE GOALS

Priority	Goals	Date Needed	Cost Estimate	Amount Already Saved	How to Achieve ($ per month, second job, etc.)

MIDDLE-RANGE/LONG-RANGE GOALS

Priority	Goals	Date Needed	Cost Estimate	Amount Already Saved	How to Achieve ($ per month, second job, etc.)

Goals Savings Record

Goal: IRA — Total Cost: 2,000

	JAN.	FEB.	MAR.	APR.	MAY	JUNE	JULY	AUG.	SEPT.	OCT.	NOV.	DEC.	
Deposit	167	167	150	160	177	167	157	177	167	167	177	167	Monthly Deposit: 167
Balance	167	334	484	644	821	988	1,145	1,322	1,489	1,656	1,833	2,000	Total: 2,000

Goal: — Total Cost:

	JAN.	FEB.	MAR.	APR.	MAY	JUNE	JULY	AUG.	SEPT.	OCT.	NOV.	DEC.	
Deposit													Monthly Deposit:
Balance													Total:

Goal: — Total Cost:

	JAN.	FEB.	MAR.	APR.	MAY	JUNE	JULY	AUG.	SEPT.	OCT.	NOV.	DEC.	
Deposit													Monthly Deposit:
Balance													Total:

Goal: — Total Cost:

	JAN.	FEB.	MAR.	APR.	MAY	JUNE	JULY	AUG.	SEPT.	OCT.	NOV.	DEC.	
Deposit													Monthly Deposit:
Balance													Total:

Goal: — Total Cost:

	JAN.	FEB.	MAR.	APR.	MAY	JUNE	JULY	AUG.	SEPT.	OCT.	NOV.	DEC.	
Deposit													Monthly Deposit:
Balance													Total:

Goal: — Total Cost:

	JAN.	FEB.	MAR.	APR.	MAY	JUNE	JULY	AUG.	SEPT.	OCT.	NOV.	DEC.	
Deposit													Monthly Deposit:
Balance													Total:

Goal: — Total Cost:

	JAN.	FEB.	MAR.	APR.	MAY	JUNE	JULY	AUG.	SEPT.	OCT.	NOV.	DEC.	
Deposit													Monthly Deposit:
Balance													Total:

Goal: — Total Cost:

	JAN.	FEB.	MAR.	APR.	MAY	JUNE	JULY	AUG.	SEPT.	OCT.	NOV.	DEC.	
Deposit													Monthly Deposit:
Balance													Total:

Goal: — Total Cost:

	JAN.	FEB.	MAR.	APR.	MAY	JUNE	JULY	AUG.	SEPT.	OCT.	NOV.	DEC.	
Deposit													Monthly Deposit:
Balance													Total:

The formula for determining the monthly amount to save for each of your goals is:
Total cost of your goal ÷ Number of months left to date needed = Amount per month need to save.

Needs/Wants List

TAKING FURTHER CONTROL OF FINANCES

This Needs/Wants List is like a "wish list" that helps you take financial control one step further. This section is designed to be a guideline for those times when you have extra money but want to be sure that you wisely use your money on priority items versus impulse items.

NEEDS AND WANTS VERSUS GOALS

Needs, wants and goals as used in this book are all the things that you would like to have but must wait until you can afford them. With your improved budgeting skills and money awareness, you know you will have the capability to eventually acquire these items.

The difference between needs/wants and goals is primarily in the cost and the significance of the desired items. Goals are more significant plans involving time and the gradual accumulation of funds for major purchases such as a computer, car or home. Elimination of a major debt is also a goal.

Needs and wants, on the other hand, are the smaller-ticket items. These are the purchases made when extra money (known as discretionary money) is left over after paying the bills and putting money aside for your savings and your goals.

HOW TO USE THIS LIST

Throughout the year, you probably see or think about many things you need or would like to have, but don't have the extra cash at the time to buy them. Jot down all your ideas on this Needs/Wants List.

Items on your list can range from things seen in mail-order catalogs, TV advertisements or stores to activities such as the opera, a concert or a ski weekend. Having these ideas written down also will make it easier for you to remember to watch for sales and list gift ideas as they come up.

At the same time, make a check mark either under the "Need" (necessities for your everyday well-being such as food, rent or medicine) or "Want" (which are nice to have, such as tapes, jewelry or theater tickets, but which you can do without if you have to) column. This way, you can make sure you take care of needs first when extra money is available. Record the source and cost of your items. When you are ready to purchase the listed item, the necessary information will be handy.

By using this Needs/Wants List, you start establishing priorities and identifying what you really do want when you have extra money. When you have an extra $50 (which you determine after completing your Monthly Budget Worksheet in Part Two) and a sale suddenly catches your eye, you won't be so apt to impulsively buy something. It will be easier to remember that there was something else you really wanted or needed when extra money is available.

A FAMILY AFFAIR

The ability to prioritize is a valuable skill for all age levels. If your children ask for something when money is tight, write down their wishes on the list or have the children write them down. Your action assures your children that you are acknowledging their needs and wants rather than saying that they just can't have something. In this way, children also learn to establish priorities, make choices and develop patience. When money does become available, either from your budget or from their gifts or other money sources, your children can choose which item on the list to buy based on cost and priority instead of reacting impulsively to the first temptation that catches their eye in the store.

PARENTS

Date	Item	Need	Want	Source (store, catalog, other)	Cost

CHILDREN

Date	Item	Need	Want	Source (store, catalog, other)	Cost

Part Two

Yearly Budget Worksheet
Gift Giving Worksheet
Christmas Holiday Expense Worksheet

Monthly Budget Worksheet
Credit Card Purchase Record
Debt Payoff Record

Monthly Expense Record
Summary for the Year Record

A*s a student, I used to carry my workbook with me every day in my pack. For anyone not used to figures, this workbook is an easy way to start. When I wrote things down every day it made me think, "Do I really need this?" "Where could I save?" "Is there something I'd rather spend my money on?" Writing everything down and seeing the total picture clearly gave me those answers and a real incentive to change.*

Now that you are ready to develop a spending plan (a budget), let me walk you through the process just as if I were sitting with you at your dining room table, as I do with my clients.

The three boldface sections above, the **Yearly Budget Worksheet, Monthly Budget Worksheet,** and **Monthly Expense Record,** form the keystone for the whole budgeting process for all households. The other forms are supplemental worksheets for households with different financial needs. Over the years as I have worked with clients and talked with readers using this workbook,

I have found that using these three sections in this order has provided the most significant results.

For years readers have had their favorite sections. Some used only one or two sections, where others used nearly all of them. The purpose of this revised workbook is still to give you the same flexibility to pick and choose the sections that will work best for you. However, I want you to have the opportunity to understand the sections early on so you don't overlook one that could be particularly valuable for you.

The **Yearly Budget Worksheet** is the worksheet that I have found makes all the difference in the world for people, right from the beginning. By starting with this overall yearly picture of where your money goes above and beyond the regular monthly bills and expenses, you see immediately and graphically why you are usually short each month, why you have so little to show for all the good money you make, or why your debt never seems to go down each year.

The **Monthly Budget Worksheet** is the next critical tool. As you begin each new month use this worksheet to streamline the whole bill paying and budget planning process. This form helps you to anticipate all the bills as well as the majority of incidental expenses (hair perm, son's field trip, photo developing, etc.) so you know and can project ahead of time (before the month even begins) how much money you will need for the entire month. You will immediately see if you are going to be short so you have time to start making some arrangements and changes. You will also know what you can and cannot afford in terms of impulsive splurge events.

The **Monthly Expense Record** lets you know where all your money has really gone for the whole month. This is your reality check on what your spending habits (like the coffee and donuts, CDs and tapes, etc.) are actually costing you.

I would be lost without my workbook. It's my bible. By keeping it next to the coffee and kids' money for school, the workbook is always handy. I color-code expenses for my kids and under pets I highlight the expenses of the horses in yellow and dogs in red so I know the real cost of each.

Yearly Budget Worksheet (Nonmonthly Anticipated Expenses)

WHY A YEARLY BUDGET WORKSHEET?

This worksheet is designed to give you a general yearly overview of your irregular, occasional, non-monthly expenses at a glance. This method often provides a more manageable approach than the use of files, notes on the calendar or even some software programs.

Having this information can prevent those pay periods when you finally have all the bills paid and give a sigh of relief only to be deluged the next day with auto insurance and property tax bills you had overlooked or not anticipated, which put your whole budget in a tailspin once again.

By having all this information as early in the year as possible, you can use it to make necessary arrangements ahead of time. How much money should you put aside for the dental work, could you postpone that new sofa, how can the vacation be less costly, is it time to cut back on the gifts? By thinking these options through ahead of time and taking action, you won't be falling back on the credit cards or loans to get you through the year.

FILLING IN YOUR YEARLY BUDGET WORKSHEET

Be patient as you go through this first form. It will require more time initially. However, the insights and information you gain will be well worth your time. Once this worksheet is completed, it becomes a valuable reference page for the remainder of the year.

To get started, grab your pencil, eraser, and calculator. Then gather up your check book registers, insurance papers, credit card statements, and any other related household papers which may give the exact or estimated amounts of expenses plus the months these expenses are due or paid.

Start at the top left, look at the expense category and if it applies to you, move across the page to the right and fill in the exact or estimated amount under the month or months the expense is due. I suggest pencil because as you work this through, changes and new additions will come up.

See the Suggestion List at the end of these instructions to find additional and often overlooked expenses which may apply to your household but are not on this worksheet. The worksheet is deliberately kept quite generic so you can adjust it to your own unique needs.

For those expense categories where you really don't have a clue what the cost will be, guess. That's right. It is okay not to be perfect and it is also more valuable to keep moving through this exercise than to use the missing information as a reason to stop or get discouraged. You are already going through the most important process by thinking about these expenses and filling in most of the information. You can always add to this section later as new or more accurate information becomes available.

ADDITIONAL NOTES ABOUT THE CATEGORIES

This worksheet is a guideline for you. You may find you have to add or cross out and replace certain categories. Remember to do whatever works best for your unique financial picture.

This section will be especially helpful if you are on a very tight budget this year. Some of your expenses like insurance or taxes will be fixed where there will be no room for negotiating or eliminating this expense.

On the other hand, a number of the expenses may not be so immediate nor be considered "needs," but are still preferred when the extra money is available. When you have the whole picture in front of you and see the total cost it will be easier to make decisions about how to handle those expenses when the money is still tight.

Be sure to check in with the Suggestion List so you totally take advantage of this worksheet and include all the valuable information that belongs here. Below are a few notes for some of the categories.

Home/Yard Maintenance can include expenses that range from a new mattress to an addition to the house or back yard. If you have been thinking about new furniture and have been trying to decide when you can afford it, use this Yearly Budget Worksheet for your planning.

Auto Expense is much like the medical. If you stop to think this area through ahead of time you can estimate when you might need tires or need to take your car in for its 60,000-mile checkup.

Medical Expenses are often difficult to know in advance, yet it is helpful to think about the different areas on the Suggestion List ahead of time so you start to anticipate a possible expense rather than react to it. Put some estimate down, even the small co-pays, to remind you of the expenses throughout the year.

Vacations can be planned in advance. Keep in mind the mini-weekend trip as well as those holiday and summer vacations. Both gifts and vacations are good practice places for learning to live within your income. You may enjoy buying expensive gifts or going on exotic vacations, but if this puts a hardship on your budget, you may have to reevaluate your priorities. Either spend less on these categories or less on some other categories.

Gifts, for some households, are a minimal expense. Yet for others who place a high priority on gifts, the gift expense area can be a major expense when remembering Christmas, birthdays, weddings, Mother's and Father's Days, anniversaries, baby showers, graduation, etc. Planning all this information out ahead of time will make it all more manageable.

The Gift Giving Worksheet is a separate worksheet to use for outlining all the gifts you plan to give throughout the year. You can total the amounts for each month and transfer those totals to the "Gift" category on this worksheet. Even though Christmas gifts are often purchased throughout the year, I do suggest putting the whole Christmas gift expense total under December only to keep this planning simple.

Holiday Events vary from household to household depending on how you celebrate Valentine's Day, July 4th, Halloween, Thanksgiving, and other traditional and religious events in your family. Don't forget the cost of decorating the house or purchasing a new Halloween costume along with all the other related expenses. By listing these estimates as well as the others on this page, you will have a more realistic approach to all your upcoming expenses.

I *started using your book when it got to the point where we just didn't know where all the money was going. I figured most of it was going to meals out, which turned out to be true, but what shocked me was the amount being spent on gifts!*

The **Christmas Holiday Expense Worksheet** can help you fine-tune the real expense of Christmas on top of the gift expense. Many of my clients will guess an amount for this category. Then when we work through the real estimate with the worksheet, the total amount is usually three times their guess.

All of these various expenses are just more examples of "where the money goes."

HOW TO USE THIS INFORMATION

Once you have taken time to estimate and project your upcoming nonmonthly expenses, you have valuable information that graphically shows you which months will be light and which ones will be difficult to deal with. At this point you can evaluate each expense and consider your choices; you can cut back, postpone, modify, or eliminate the expense. Which choice best fits your personal needs?

When you total up all of these expenses, you can quickly see why there never seems to be enough money. This is where the Reserve Savings Account mentioned earlier in the discussion on savings now makes more sense. When you total these expenses and divide by 12 (to get your monthly average) you can see how much money must be put aside each month to prepare for these upcoming expenses. You then can transfer this amount onto the **Monthly Budget Worksheet** page and list it as Reserve Savings to help you plan ahead for the month.

As you look at this completed worksheet, what does it tell you? First, as mentioned above, you can see which months are going to be high stress months and which ones will be workable light months. Now you have a guideline to let you know which month would be better when taking on additional expenses.

Second, you can see what you ideally need to put aside each month to save up for all these expenses. If that amount is too much at this time, pick some of the fixed and most expensive categories like property tax, gifts, auto repairs, etc., and start putting aside one twelfth of those totals. You can also use the Goals Saving Record in Part One or the general Savings Record in Part Three to help track your savings.

Third, and most significantly, that monthly average amount is how much you are "affected" indirectly each month by these expenses. This effect or impact usually shows up in the form of added credit card debt, more or larger loans, financial juggling, doing without, and overall frustration.

Now that you can see this and realize what has been happening to your overall budget each year, you can do something about it. That's the exciting part. As one woman said, "I'm depressed and excited at the same time!"

REMINDER

This worksheet is your guideline and is meant to be as flexible as possible. You are the one who decides how to utilize the worksheet and the information to your best advantage.

Suggestion List—Additional Nonmonthly Expenses

You can either complete this information here and then transfer it to the Yearly Budget Worksheet or use this as your guideline as you fill in the worksheet directly from these ideas.

Some of the expenses listed may be a monthly expense for you. If so, enter those expenses on the Monthly Budget Worksheet, not here. The focus of the Yearly Budget Worksheet is only on the periodic, quarterly, semiannual, annual, and nonmonthly expenses.

	Description	Amount/s	Months Due
Housing	Property Taxes		
	Home Insurance		
	Association/Condo Dues		
	Yard/Garden Supplies		
	Yard Service/Maintenance		
	Pool Chemicals/Maintenance		
	Exterminator		
	Security System		
	Home Improvement Projects		
	Home Repairs/Maintenance		
	Carpet Cleaning		
	Window Cleaning		
	Dry Cleaning (Drapes, Bedding)		
	Furniture/Appliances/Electronics		
	Maintenance Agreements		
	Other _____		
Utilities (Nonmonthly)	Fuel/Propane		
	Firewood		
	Waste Management		
	Water/Water Softener		
	Other _____		
Transportation	Vehicle #1 Insurance		
	Vehicle #2 Insurance		
	Boat/RV/Motorcycle Insurance		
	Emission Inspection		
	License Renewal		
	Oil Changes		
	Other Maintenance and Repairs		
	Other _____		
Health	Contact Lens Insurance		
	Other Insurance		
	Medical Exams/Lab Tests		
	Visits (Sick Kids/Allergy/etc.)		
	Physical Exam		
	Prescriptions		
	Chiropractor		
	Dermatologist		
	Dental Exams/X rays/Cleanings		
	Dental Work Needed		
	Orthodontia		
	Vision Exam/Glasses/Contacts		
	Alternative Health Practitioners		
	Vitamins/Supplements/Homeopathic		
	Other _____		

	Description	Amount/s	Months Due
Insur-ance (Other)	Life Insurance Disability Insurance Other _____		
Memberships	Church Country Club Credit Card Annual Fees Gym Annual Fees Organizations/Clubs Professional Dues Professional License Sports Warehouse Clubs Other _____		
Education (Adult)	Tuition Book/Supply Expense Computer Equipment/Maintenance Trade Journals/Magazines/Newspaper Workshop/Seminar/Speakers Other _____		
Clothing (Adults and Children)	Work Clothes/Uniforms/Shoes Seasonal Clothes/Shoes/Jackets Sports Clothes/Special Events Dry Clean/Alterations/Shoe Repair		
Recreation (Adults)	Season Tickets Concerts/Sports Events Fees: Permits/Tournament/League Hobbies/Sports Equipment and Maintenance Lessons Other _____		
Vacation/ Trips	Transportation Lodging/Meals/Snacks Sights/Activities Shopping/Souvenirs		
Children	Tuition Back to School Supplies Photos/Yearbooks/Class Ring/Letter Jacket Prom/Homecoming (Flowers, Hair, Dinner etc.) Field Trips/Contests/Expos/Fund Raising Camp Registration/Supplies Sports Equipment/Fees/Clinics Music Lessons/Equipment/Recitals/Costumes Other _____		
Pets	Pet Food Grooming Vet Expense License Training Pet Hotel Other _____		
Misc.	Donations Tax Preparation Taxes Due Retirement Savings (IRA)		

Yearly Budget Worksheet **19**

FIXED AND ESTIMATED NONMONTHLY EXPENSES

	JAN.	FEB.	MAR.	APR.	MAY	JUNE	JULY	AUG.	SEPT.	OCT.	NOV.	DEC.	TOTAL	MO. AVE.
Property Tax / Home Insurance														
Home/Yard Maintenance			Door 250	Yard 150			Drapes 250						650	54
Utilities *Sewer*			65		20				50			85	220	18
Auto Insurance *Van* / *Car*			Van 500 / Car 425						500 / 425				1,000 / 850	154
Auto Expenses		Lube 25	Tires 250		Lube 25			Lube 25	Lic. 100	Lic. 80	Tune up 150		655	55
Insurance—Other *Life*		80		80				80			80		320	27
Medical Expenses	Rx 75		250	Dr. A. 20				Rx 75			Lab 70		490	41
Dental/Vision Expense		Dental 750				Vis. 300		Dental 75					1,125	94
Dues/Fees *Taxes*		Prof. Lic. 95		Tax Prep 300		Fish. 35	AAA 35	License 130			AMEX 55		650	54
Education/Tuition *Student Loan*		85	Seminar 150		85			85	Seminar 100		85		590	49
Clothing - *Child*	Shoes/Coat 320				350			400					1,070	89
Recreation	Concert 60				Fish Lic. 35				Season Ticket 75				170	14
Vacation/Trips		Ski 250				800					300		1,350	112
Magazines		YM 16			Kip 20							BL 39	75	6
Gifts—Birthday	25	15	50			15	100			100	75		380	32
Gifts—Other	Anniv. 40		Grad. M. Day 50	60	F. Day 30			Shower 35	Wedding 40			Xmas 700	955	80
Holiday Events			Easter 25				40		Halloween 60		TG 70	Xmas 400	595	50
Children's Activities	65		Field trip 100			Camp 150	Lessons 65		School 75	Photos 50			505	42
Pets														
Donations		15	WWF 25				G.P. 30			RC 50		CRS 100	220	18
Personal	Perm 80			25			Perm 80			25			210	18
Total	680	1,316	1,965	600	725	1,350	600	905	1,225	505	885	1,324	12,080	1,007

Reserve Savings: Total Expenses $ _12,080_ ÷ 12 = $ _1,006.67_ /month   *Rounded Up*

FIXED AND ESTIMATED NONMONTHLY EXPENSES

	JAN.	FEB.	MAR.	APR.	MAY	JUNE	JULY	AUG.	SEPT.	OCT.	NOV.	DEC.	TOTAL	MO. AVE.
Property Tax Home Insurance														
Home/Yard Maintenance														
Utilities														
Auto Insurance														
Auto Expenses														
Insurance—Other														
Medical Expenses														
Dental/Vision Expense														
Dues/Fees														
Education/Tuition														
Clothing														
Recreation														
Vacation/Trips														
Gifts—Birthday														
Gifts—Other														
Holiday Events														
Children's Activities														
Pets														
Total														

Reserve
Savings: Total Expenses $_____ ÷ 12 = $_____/month

Gift Giving Worksheet

Gift giving is often one of the most underestimated and overlooked budget categories in many households. People often are amazed, once they start recording all their expenses, just how much money actually is spent on gifts. It is not uncommon to forget occasional events or extended family members or teachers, bosses, hair-dressers, and pets on this gift list when trying to estimate the overall gift budget.

This Gift Giving Worksheet works as a reminder as you anticipate the total yearly cost for all upcoming events involving gifts. Remembering Christmas and birthdays generally is easy. Events such as Father's Day

Gift Giving Worksheet

	Name	Amount: Christmas/ Hanukkah	Birthday	(Month Due)	Other*	(Month Due)
Parents						
Children						
Sisters/Brothers						
Friends/Other						

*Other: Anniversaries, weddings, showers, new babies, Mother's Day, Father's Day, graduation, religious events.

or your parents' anniversary, however, often are over-looked until the month they occur. Even if you don't buy gifts but send flowers or go out to dinner instead, include these costs in your plan. By outlining all the members of your family and your friends and all the events cel-ebrated in your household on this worksheet, you have a handy total picture of what gift expenses to expect. You then can transfer these amounts to the "Gifts" section of the Yearly Budget Worksheet under the appropriate months.

Gift Giving Worksheet

	Name	Amount: Christmas/ Hanukkah	Birthday	(Month Due)	Other*	(Month Due)
Grandparents						
Aunts/Uncles						
Nieces/Nephews						
Children's Friends						

*Other: Anniversaries, weddings, showers, new babies, Mother's Day, Father's Day, graduation, religious events.

Christmas/Holiday Expense Worksheet

Item	Estimate	Already Have	Actual Cost
Tree/Wreath			
Lights—House/Tree			
Bake Goods/Ginger House Parties/Food/Liquor			
Poinsettias/Candles Decorations/Crafts			
Gift Wrap Greeting Cards			
Postage Shipping/Boxes			
Photo Development Family Portraits			
Clothes/Shoes/Jewelry			
Meals Out			
Movies/Ballet/Play Travel/Tour			
Donations			
Batteries/Misc. (Gifts) Other			
Total Amount	$		$

Source of Money for Gifts and Holiday Expenses

Total Amount for Gifts:
(See Gift Giving Worksheet) $ _____

Total Amount—Expenses:
(See Worksheet at Left) $ _____

TOTAL AMOUNT NEEDED: $ _____

How Much Is Available from the Following Sources to Cover These Expenses:

Source	Amount	Notes
Current Income		
Extra Hours/ Part-time Job		
Savings Account		
Gift Money/ Bonus		
Put On Charge Cards		
Borrow		
Total Amount	$	

Monthly Budget Worksheet

WHY A MONTHLY BUDGET WORKSHEET?

The Monthly Budget Worksheet is designed to provide a guideline for coordinating your monthly bills and expenses with your take-home pay. Your monthly bills are often easier to remember because most bills often come in the mail. Forgotten, however, are the expenses each month such as meals eaten out, haircuts, gifts, books, tapes, seminars, etc., which often throw off the monthly budget.

This worksheet is especially helpful during those lean times when work hours are reduced and the amount of bills to pay exceeds the money coming in. This guideline will give you a better overall picture of your monthly obligations and lifestyle expenses. The categories are kept general to allow for flexibility and necessary additions based on your own personal financial needs.

Often something as simple as this worksheet can be the difference between financial chaos and financial control. For the Mathews the true test came when the commission check was exceptionally low one month. After months of working diligently on their budget, this young ambitious couple had the skills and tools to tighten up and be creative about their spending. They knew what to do. Banana bread was made at home to replace the sales meeting bagels, all meals out were eliminated, brown bag meals and soggy sandwiches replaced the business meals out while on the road and all other discretionary spending was cut back. By the end of the month the Mathews were ecstatic as they made it through the month financially intact—all the bills were paid, good meals were eaten at home, no credit card charges, no little loans, and best of all,

they felt totally motivated by their ability to take control of the situation.

WHAT TO DO WITH THAT STACK OF BILLS

To use the Monthly Budget Worksheet, write the net amounts of each paycheck in the blanks at the top on the "Net Income Total Amount" line. You will notice the ① emphasis on net income and not on gross income throughout this workbook. This way, you are dealing only with the cash you actually have for paying your bills. (See the **Monthly Expense Record** for information regarding payroll deductions and taxes.) How many columns under "Income Source" you fill in depends on how often you are paid each month. Of course, there are many job situations where the amount may vary or is not always known, such as with sales commissions. If this is the case, make a very *conservative* estimate until the actual amount is known.

Under the "Income Source" amount, there is room ② to add the date each paycheck is received. This will help with your planning when working with due dates on the bills.

Next, divide the bills into two stacks: one for those that must be paid that month and another for those bills that can be postponed if necessary. Look at the amounts of the "must" bills and write their amounts in the appropriate blanks under the "Income Source" according to the due dates or other deadlines. At this point, you may want or need to make arrangements ahead of time with the respective companies for partial or late payments for those bills you are unable to pay on time.

Try to distribute and balance the more expensive bills over the different pay periods rather than pay them all with one check. If you have enough money to handle more than the "must" bills, now is the time to distribute the amount of the "postponable" bills under the "Income Source."

PAY YOURSELF FIRST

③   Notice that "Allowance/Mad Money" and "Savings" are under "Fixed Amounts." The phrase "Pay yourself first" has been said many times. It is a valid statement and a very important rule because if you penny-pinch to the point where there is no money left for "Allowance/Mad Money," you will end up bickering, frustrated, and disappointed with the whole budget idea. The "Allowance/Mad Money" should be yours to do with as you please. You must decide how much "Allowance/Mad Money" each member needs to allow for little splurges and yet not ignore the necessary expenses.

Just as important under "Fixed Amounts" is "Savings." Again, this is paying yourself first. Consider "Savings" as an *expense,* setting aside a specific amount or percentage of your check at the same time you are completing the other categories of the worksheet. In this manner, you will be thinking of "Savings" as an expense so that it is planned for regularly and not dependent on leftover funds.

Remember the different savings accounts: **reserve** (for upcoming known bills and expenses listed on the **Yearly Budget Worksheet**), **emergency** (equivalent to three months of take-home pay for unknown disasters) and **goals** (wish list) and try to save regularly for them. Once you have saved enough money for the reserve and emergency accounts, you will realize that it is actually possible to save money. Saving for your goals soon becomes more exciting and challenging as you realize that reaching your goals now is possible.

NOW FOR SOME PRACTICE AT BUDGETING

In many cases, such as utilities or other areas under "Fixed Variable" and "Occasional," the exact amount of the bill is unknown. For those categories, a space for ④ "Budget" has been included. This is where your budgeting practice comes in. This space can be used to help plan for the bills until the exact amount is known. Remember to keep in mind those other expenses that are not seen as bills but show up on a daily basis: food, gas,

entertainment, clothing, etc. Those must be planned for as well. Here you will take an estimated guess (budget) as to what you will need and the amount you can spend. If you use the **Monthly Expense Record** for tracking your expenses each month you will have a better sense of some averages to use for these categories when estimating. Once you become familiar with estimating your expenditures, you will successfully begin to live within your budget. If your budget is realistic, you soon will choose to do without certain unnecessary items to remain within the projected budget.

THE TIME FOR REEVALUATION

Finally, complete the "Totals" at the bottom of the ⑤ page. After determining all the totals, you may have some columns that have more total bills than income and some columns that have more income than bills. Try to rearrange the bills to be paid to different columns so there will be a balance.

During some periods, no matter how much you rearrange the bills or postpone the bills to the last possible day, it still is impossible to pay them with only your paycheck. This is the time for some real evaluation. You must decide what you need to change or do without to live within your income. Go over the budgeted expenses such as personal, clothing, etc., to see if any of these costs can be postponed, cut back or eliminated. Contact the companies to make special payment arrangements. Many companies (utilities, medical clinics, department stores, etc.) are very willing to accommodate you if you will notify them and make partial payments.

What else can you do? How can you bring more money in? Can you get more overtime hours or a part-time job? Do you have enough "stuff" to have a yard sale? What if you took your unused books, CDs, and clothes to the resale shops for some extra cash?

In the meantime, possibly you have been building a small emergency fund and can cover expenses this time by withdrawing the necessary amount. This should be an absolute last resort, however, with cutbacks planned for the next few months so that you can replenish your emergency fund again.

GETTING CONTROL OF YOUR FINANCES

You have just completed an important step in getting and keeping control of your finances. Of course, doing a Monthly Budget Worksheet does not change or increase the amount of actual money earned. Being aware, however, of where and how the money is spent will give you the feeling that you are beginning to control your money and will help you stretch the use of those dollars more than before.

Happy Budgeting!

I was shocked into action when I worked out my budget on the Monthly Budget Worksheet and realized I was $1,000 short. Now after four years all our bills are paid in full and we are completely out of debt. Without putting information down on paper every month I don't think I could have done it.

Monthly Budget Worksheet   SAMPLE

INCOME SOURCE:			Income	Income	Income	Income	Reserve Savings
① Net Income Total Amount:			896	1,407	880	1,407	1,380
Expenses		④ Budget	Date: 9/4 ②	9/7	9/18	9/21	9/15

	Expenses	④ Budget	9/4	9/7	9/18	9/21	9/15
Fixed Amounts	Mortgage/Rent	784	784				
	Car Payments	291		291			
	Other Loans student	167		167			
	Day Care						
	Insurance Auto	500*					500
	Auto	425*					425
	Club/Dues						
	Emerg.	215				115	
	Goals	75		100		75	
	Savings Reserve	1,007		400	300	307	
③	Allowance/Mad Money	50	20		30		
Fixed Variable	Electricity	75			75		
	Fuel/Gas	45			45		
	Water/Garbage	125*					125
	Telephone	65			65		
	Cable TV	35			35		
	Food	450	50	150	50	200	
	Meals Out	125		30	50	45	
	Auto Expense/Gas	85		30	30	25	
	Auto License	100*					100
	activities	30					
	child allowance	40	10	10	10	40	
	Church/Charity	325		70		255	
Occasional	Household Photos	20			20		
	Personal Perm	80*					80
	Clothes /Dry Clean	75 / 35	25	35		50	
	Medical Prescrip.	35		35			
	Child Expense School Exp.	75*					75
	Recreation Season Ticket	75*					75
	Counseling	130		65		65	
	Books, CDs	35	10		25		
Installment	Credit Cards Movies/videos	55		25		30	
	Visa	100			100		
	MC	200				200	
⑤	**Total Expense** Excludes*	4,549	899	1,408	835	1,407	1,380
	Total Income	4,590					
	Total Excess	41			45		
	Total Short		−3	−1			

Paid from Reserve Savings (Yearly Budget Worksheet) and not included in this Total Expense figure.

INCOME SOURCE:						
Net Income Total Amount:						

	Expenses	**Budget**	**Date:**				
Fixed Amounts	Mortgage/Rent						
	Car Payments						
	Other Loans						
	Day Care						
	Insurance						
	Club/Dues						
	Savings						
	Allowance/Mad Money						
Fixed Variable	Electricity						
	Fuel/Gas						
	Water/Garbage						
	Telephone						
	Cable TV						
	Food						
	Meals Out						
	Auto Expense/Gas						
	Church/Charity						
Occasional	Household						
	Personal						
	Clothes						
	Medical						
	Child Expense						
	Recreation						
Installment	Credit Cards						
Total	**Total Expense**						
	Total Income						
	Total Excess						
	Total Short						

	INCOME SOURCE:						
	Net Income Total Amount:						
	Expenses	**Budget**	**Date:**				
Fixed Amounts	Mortgage/Rent						
	Car Payments						
	Other Loans						
	Day Care						
	Insurance						
	Club/Dues						
	Savings						
	Allowance/Mad Money						
Fixed Variable	Electricity						
	Fuel/Gas						
	Water/Garbage						
	Telephone						
	Cable TV						
	Food						
	Meals Out						
	Auto Expense/Gas						
	Church/Charity						
Occasional	Household						
	Personal						
	Clothes						
	Medical						
	Child Expense						
	Recreation						
Installment	Credit Cards						
Total	**Total Expense**						
	Total Income						
	Total Excess						
	Total Short						

INCOME SOURCE:						
Net Income Total Amount:						

	Expenses	**Budget**	**Date:**				
Fixed Amounts	Mortgage/Rent						
	Car Payments						
	Other Loans						
	Day Care						
	Insurance						
	Club/Dues						
	Savings						
	Allowance/Mad Money						
Fixed Variable	Electricity						
	Fuel/Gas						
	Water/Garbage						
	Telephone						
	Cable TV						
	Food						
	Meals Out						
	Auto Expense/Gas						
	Church/Charity						
Occasional	Household						
	Personal						
	Clothes						
	Medical						
	Child Expense						
	Recreation						
Installment	Credit Cards						
Total	**Total Expense**						
	Total Income						
	Total Excess						
	Total Short						

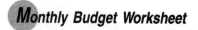
INCOME SOURCE:						
Net Income Total Amount:						

	Expenses	Budget	Date:			
Fixed Amounts	Mortgage/Rent					
	Car Payments					
	Other Loans					
	Day Care					
	Insurance					
	Club/Dues					
	Savings					
	Allowance/Mad Money					
Fixed Variable	Electricity					
	Fuel/Gas					
	Water/Garbage					
	Telephone					
	Cable TV					
	Food					
	Meals Out					
	Auto Expense/Gas					
	Church/Charity					
Occasional	Household					
	Personal					
	Clothes					
	Medical					
	Child Expense					
	Recreation					
Installment	Credit Cards					
Total	**Total Expense**					
	Total Income					
	Total Excess					
	Total Short					

INCOME SOURCE:						
Net Income Total Amount:						

	Expenses	Budget	Date:				
Fixed Amounts	Mortgage/Rent						
	Car Payments						
	Other Loans						
	Day Care						
	Insurance						
	Club/Dues						
	Savings						
	Allowance/Mad Money						
Fixed Variable	Electricity						
	Fuel/Gas						
	Water/Garbage						
	Telephone						
	Cable TV						
	Food						
	Meals Out						
	Auto Expense/Gas						
	Church/Charity						
Occasional	Household						
	Personal						
	Clothes						
	Medical						
	Child Expense						
	Recreation						
Installment	Credit Cards						
Total	**Total Expense**						
	Total Income						
	Total Excess						
	Total Short						

INCOME SOURCE:						
Net Income Total Amount:						

	Expenses	**Budget**	**Date:**				
Fixed Amounts	Mortgage/Rent						
	Car Payments						
	Other Loans						
	Day Care						
	Insurance						
	Club/Dues						
	Savings						
	Allowance/Mad Money						
Fixed Variable	Electricity						
	Fuel/Gas						
	Water/Garbage						
	Telephone						
	Cable TV						
	Food						
	Meals Out						
	Auto Expense/Gas						
	Church/Charity						
Occasional	Household						
	Personal						
	Clothes						
	Medical						
	Child Expense						
	Recreation						
Installment	Credit Cards						
Total	**Total Expense**						
	Total Income						
	Total Excess						
	Total Short						

Monthly Budget Worksheet

INCOME SOURCE:						
Net Income Total Amount:						
	Expenses	**Budget**	**Date:**			

	Expenses	Budget	Date:			
Fixed Amounts	Mortgage/Rent					
	Car Payments					
	Other Loans					
	Day Care					
	Insurance					
	Club/Dues					
	Savings					
	Allowance/Mad Money					
Fixed Variable	Electricity					
	Fuel/Gas					
	Water/Garbage					
	Telephone					
	Cable TV					
	Food					
	Meals Out					
	Auto Expense/Gas					
	Church/Charity					
Occasional	Household					
	Personal					
	Clothes					
	Medical					
	Child Expense					
	Recreation					
Installment	Credit Cards					
Total	**Total Expense**					
	Total Income					
	Total Excess					
	Total Short					

Monthly Budget Worksheet

	Expenses	Budget	Date:				
	INCOME SOURCE:						
	Net Income Total Amount:						
Fixed Amounts	Mortgage/Rent						
	Car Payments						
	Other Loans						
	Day Care						
	Insurance						
	Club/Dues						
	Savings						
	Allowance/Mad Money						
Fixed Variable	Electricity						
	Fuel/Gas						
	Water/Garbage						
	Telephone						
	Cable TV						
	Food						
	Meals Out						
	Auto Expense/Gas						
	Church/Charity						
Occasional	Household						
	Personal						
	Clothes						
	Medical						
	Child Expense						
	Recreation						
Installment	Credit Cards						
Total	**Total Expense**						
	Total Income						
	Total Excess						
	Total Short						

INCOME SOURCE:						
Net Income Total Amount:						

	Expenses	Budget	Date:				
Fixed Amounts	Mortgage/Rent						
	Car Payments						
	Other Loans						
	Day Care						
	Insurance						
	Club/Dues						
	Savings						
	Allowance/Mad Money						
Fixed Variable	Electricity						
	Fuel/Gas						
	Water/Garbage						
	Telephone						
	Cable TV						
	Food						
	Meals Out						
	Auto Expense/Gas						
	Church/Charity						
Occasional	Household						
	Personal						
	Clothes						
	Medical						
	Child Expense						
	Recreation						
Installment	Credit Cards						
Total	**Total Expense**						
	Total Income						
	Total Excess						
	Total Short						

INCOME SOURCE:							
Net Income Total Amount:							

	Expenses	Budget	Date:				
Fixed Amounts	Mortgage/Rent						
	Car Payments						
	Other Loans						
	Day Care						
	Insurance						
	Club/Dues						
	Savings						
	Allowance/Mad Money						
Fixed Variable	Electricity						
	Fuel/Gas						
	Water/Garbage						
	Telephone						
	Cable TV						
	Food						
	Meals Out						
	Auto Expense/Gas						
	Church/Charity						
Occasional	Household						
	Personal						
	Clothes						
	Medical						
	Child Expense						
	Recreation						
Installment	Credit Cards						
Total	**Total Expense**						
	Total Income						
	Total Excess						
	Total Short						

 **M**onthly Budget Worksheet

INCOME SOURCE:						
Net Income Total Amount:						

	Expenses	Budget	Date:				
Fixed Amounts	Mortgage/Rent						
	Car Payments						
	Other Loans						
	Day Care						
	Insurance						
	Club/Dues						
	Savings						
	Allowance/Mad Money						
Fixed Variable	Electricity						
	Fuel/Gas						
	Water/Garbage						
	Telephone						
	Cable TV						
	Food						
	Meals Out						
	Auto Expense/Gas						
	Church/Charity						
Occasional	Household						
	Personal						
	Clothes						
	Medical						
	Child Expense						
	Recreation						
Installment	Credit Cards						
Total	Total Expense						
	Total Income						
	Total Excess						
	Total Short						

	Expenses	Budget	Date:				
INCOME SOURCE:							
	Net Income Total Amount:						
Fixed Amounts	Mortgage/Rent						
	Car Payments						
	Other Loans						
	Day Care						
	Insurance						
	Club/Dues						
	Savings						
	Allowance/Mad Money						
Fixed Variable	Electricity						
	Fuel/Gas						
	Water/Garbage						
	Telephone						
	Cable TV						
	Food						
	Meals Out						
	Auto Expense/Gas						
	Church/Charity						
Occasional	Household						
	Personal						
	Clothes						
	Medical						
	Child Expense						
	Recreation						
Installment	Credit Cards						
Total	Total Expense						
	Total Income						
	Total Excess						
	Total Short						

Debt Payoff Record

In two years' time we went from $16,000 debt to $2,000 (vehicles) and saved over $10,000. It took facing the numbers in the workbook, seeing what we spent every day, realizing how much money was going to finance charges, and getting out of our denial about debt. Now we still buy clothes and go on vacations. The difference is the planning and saving ahead of time.

WHEN TO USE THIS WORKSHEET

If you are beginning to get deep in debt or just need a better idea of how much you still owe on all your bills such as medical expenses, car loan, finance company loan, credit cards, department store cards, etc., this worksheet is an important step for regaining financial control.

Staying organized is easier as well, as you now have a way to keep all your credit information in one simple place. You can also list the creditor's address and contact name, if you need this information frequently, in the blank space at the top or bottom of the page.

WHAT TO INCLUDE

The expenses to include are those you are unable to pay in full and must extend over a period of time (installment payments) such as automobile, home equity, student or finance-company loans; medical, legal, or family loans; IRS debt; and all credit card charges. This worksheet will clearly show you how much you have paid, what you still owe and how much it is costing you to pay in installments. Remember, every penny you pay for finance charges is money you could have in your pocket for savings or vacations if the bill were paid in full.

HOW TO START

Start by filling in all the information at the top of the worksheet for each debt you have. Be sure to include the Annual Percentage Rate (APR) which lets you know what interest rate you are paying.

As you make payments each month take time to actually look at your whole statement. I know the tendency is to zero in on the "Minimum Payment Due" block and ignore the rest. It's time to start paying attention to the other information on the statement like "New Balance," "Finance Charge," "Late Payment Fee," and "Over the Limit Fee." Granted, it is very difficult to acknowledge the whole picture, yet this is an important step and it is how you will begin to take charge and change your spending habits.

Fill in the "Amount Paid" and "Balance Due" for each month on this worksheet. The "Interest/Penalty" line is for all the finance charges and other fees. Just adding up that line across both pages will certainly get your attention each month.

Note how much of the minimum payment you pay is finance charge and how much is actually payment toward the balance due. Amazing, isn't it? Now you see why it is taking so long to get out of debt.

COST OF CREDIT PURCHASES

Have you ever wondered how long it would take you to pay off your credit card debt? Chart A shows an

CHART A: THE COST OF CREDIT CARD PURCHASES
BALANCE $2,000

			TOTAL COST WHEN PAYING ONLY THE MINIMUM PAYMENT				SAVINGS WHEN ADDING AN EXTRA .25/DAY TO PAYMENT		
CARD	Interest Rate	Minimum Percent Payment	Minimum Payment	Total Interest Cost	YEARS* to Payoff		Interest Paid After Extra .25/Day	Total Interest Saved	YEARS* Saved by Extra .25/Day
CARD A	19.8%	2%	$40	$7,636	42		$2,720	$4,916	28
CARD B	19.8%	2.78%	$56	$2,585	17		$1,557	$1,029	8
CARD C	12.5%	2%	$40	$1,840	18		$1,071	$ 769	8
CARD D	8.25%	3%	$60	$ 542	10		$ 400	$ 142	3

* This information was in months which was rounded up to make the extra year.

Source: *The Banker's Secret Credit Card Software.* This program makes it easy to crunch the numbers for your own credit cards, so you can see how much you can save by making payments greater than the required minimums. Available for PCs and Macs, $28 postpaid, 1-800-255-0899.

example of what you would pay if you only paid the minimum payment and then what you would pay with just an extra 25 cents a day or $7.50 a month. Chart B shows you how much you would need to pay monthly to get out of all your debt in your desired time frame.

When comparing the different minimum *percent* payments on Chart A, the smaller minimum percent (2%) certainly looks more appealing when looking at the resulting lower minimum payment ($40). Now notice how much it adds to the total interest cost and the years needed to pay off the balance. What a difference just small amounts can make.

If you can add $10 to all your minimum payments each month, you will start to see a savings of hundreds, possibly thousands each year. If you use computers you may already have the tools for calculating your savings. You can also ask your accountant, use my software *The Budget Kit CD-ROM* or use the Bankcard Holders of

CHART B: HOW SOON CAN YOU BE DEBT FREE?

The following figures are based on a debt with an average 14% interest rate.

If you want your debt paid off in the following years, see the chart below to find out how much your monthly payment would be to reach your debt free goal.

Total Debt Due	1 Yr.	2 Yr.	3 Yr.	4 Yr.	5 Yr.	6 Yr.	7 Yr.	8 Yr.	9 Yr.	10 Yr.
3,000	270	144	103	82	70	62	56	52	49	47
5,000	449	240	171	137	116	103	94	87	82	78
10,000	898	480	342	273	233	206	187	174	163	155
15,000	1,347	720	513	410	349	309	281	261	245	233
20,000	1,796	960	684	547	465	412	375	347	327	311
25,000	2,245	1,200	854	683	582	515	469	434	408	388
30,000	2,694	1,440	1,025	820	698	618	562	521	490	466
35,000	3,143	1,680	1,196	956	814	721	656	608	572	543
40,000	3,591	1,921	1,367	1,093	931	824	750	695	653	621
45,000	4,040	2,161	1,538	1,230	1,047	927	843	782	735	699
50,000	4,489	2,401	1,709	1,366	1,163	1,030	937	869	817	776
75,000	6,734	3,601	2,563	2,049	1,745	1,545	1,406	1,303	1,225	1,165

Total Monthly Payment

America "Debt Zapper" service (524 Branch Drive, Salem, VA 24153, 540-389-5445). This is a personalized repayment schedule that shaves years and often thousands of dollars off your credit card payments. For a $15 fee, Debt Zapper prioritizes your payments and calculates the most efficient way to save the most time and money.

GETTING OUT OF DEBT

After you pay off one debt, apply that same payment amount to another debt, preferably one with the highest interest, to shorten the term of that debt. An exception is if you have a smaller debt (even those with a lower interest rate) and you need the psychological satisfaction of making progress, then pay off that debt as soon as you can. As you continue to apply payments from paid-off debt to remaining debt, you will start to see how soon and how much of your total debt will be paid off in one or a few years.

By the following year, through the conscientious use of the worksheets in this workbook, you no longer may need this worksheet. Hurray! As one reader put it, "This form makes the whole workbook worth hugging a thousand times!"

GETTING CONTROL OF YOUR FINANCES

When you reach the point where you become a wise and responsible consumer and you use credit to your advantage only as a means of using someone else's money and can pay the bill in full when it is due, you will know you truly have control of your finances! You will also have much greater peace of mind.

MAKING MONEY INSTEAD OF SPENDING MONEY

Once you have gotten into the habit of making payments and applying extra money from paid-off debt to reducing the remaining debt, you will have acquired a great skill. When your debts are paid off, you can continue the payment schedule, only this time putting money into your savings and investments. All that money that was used to pay off the debt-plus-interest and penalty charges now can go toward your savings for you. Instead of spending money, you actually will be making money on the same payment amounts.

Best of all you will feel encouraged, excited and confident!

Debt Payoff Record

	Loans			Credit Cards		
CREDITOR						
Account Number						
Total Balance Due						
Phone Number						
Interest Rate (APR)						
January						
Amount Paid						
Interest/Penalty						
Balance Due						
February						
Amount Paid						
Interest/Penalty						
Balance Due						
March						
Amount Paid						
Interest/Penalty						
Balance Due						
April						
Amount Paid						
Interest/Penalty						
Balance Due						
May						
Amount Paid						
Interest/Penalty						
Balance Due						
June						
Amount Paid						
Interest/Penalty						
Balance Due						
July						
Amount Paid						
Interest/Penalty						
Balance Due						
August						
Amount Paid						
Interest/Penalty						
Balance Due						
September						
Amount Paid						
Interest/Penalty						
Balance Due						
October						
Amount Paid						
Interest/Penalty						
Balance Due						
November						
Amount Paid						
Interest/Penalty						
Balance Due						
December						
Amount Paid						
Interest/Penalty						
Balance Due						
Balance Due						

Other (Medical, Legal, Personal, etc.)

						Total

Credit Card Purchase Record

To avoid a shocking bill at the end of the month, keep careful track of your credit card charges. This way, you can anticipate what the bill will be and prepare for it by making the appropriate adjustments in your spending and your planning.

By knowing the status of your charges at all times you become much more selective and careful about impulse charging. When you reach this point, you know that you have learned how to keep from getting overextended and have taken one more step toward controlling your finances.

Credit Card Purchase Record

JAN.		FEB.		MAR.		APR.		MAY		JUNE	
Billing Cycle Closing Date: ① _____		_____		_____		_____		_____		_____	
Purchases	Amount	Purchases	Amount	Purchases	Amount	Purchases	Amount	Purchases	Amount	Purchases	Amount
③ 3/Gas ②	14.91										
7/Shoes	20.82										
Total											

HOW TO USE THIS CHART

① First find out and enter the "Billing Cycle Closing
② Date." Then record all charges made during the month
until that date so you know which purchases will be
included on that month's upcoming bill. Purchases
charged after that closing date should be entered in the
next month's column (the month for which you actually
will be billed). Jot down in the corner the date you made ③
the charge.

Remember, this chart is flexible. If you use different
cards frequently, then divide the monthly column into
the necessary parts to keep the separate records. You also
can carry an extra check register with you to record your
charges for other cards. Make the chart work for you!

Credit Card Purchase Record

JULY		AUG.		SEPT.		OCT.		NOV.		DEC.	
_____		_____		_____		_____		_____		_____	
Purchases	Amount	Purchases	Amount	Purchases	Amount	Purchases	Amount	Purchases	Amount	Purchases	Amount

Sometimes it takes the black-and-white approach to get someone's attention. Connie started using the workbook to track expenses and plan ahead when she and her husband knew they would be retiring in a few years. Her husband was staggered when he saw the expenses they both spent for six months. He was finally ready to sit down and outline and plan the finances together with Connie. They also successfully started saving for their travel plans. The workbook became an effective communication tool—a way for getting out of the dream world and back into reality.

MONTHLY EXPENSE RECORD

How many times have you asked yourself "Where did all the money go?" Even keeping detailed records in the check register does not always give a clear answer to that question. With these worksheets and with some firm self-discipline, you will easily and very graphically know exactly where all your money has gone as well as how much money has come in.

Begin by picking a time every day to jot down all the spending for that day. Some people like to carry a small notebook to record all their daily cash. Others use my *Money Tracker: A Quick and Easy Way to Keep Tabs on Your Spending* book to record cash for the week and then transfer the totals to this worksheet. With practice and determination, you will develop the habit of regularly recording all *cash, debits, checks,* and *charged* expenses. At first this may seem time-consuming and uncomfortable. However, once you get past the 21-day marker for creating a new habit, you will notice that your recording literally takes only minutes a day.

Be patient with yourself and the results. The first month or two your numbers may not be perfect, but the habit is being developed and information is emerging. By the third month you will be amazed at the results.

There is something about the act of manually recording your expenses each day (versus waiting until the end of the week or month and trying to record a pocketful of receipts) that makes a significant difference. As you physically write down the numbers, you are actually taking in a lot of information with your different senses. Visually you see all the other entries in the column and subconsciously start to note all the money already spent to date. This alone is enough to change your attitude and spending habits and help slow down the spending.

Your payoff will be the sense of control you have over your finances and finally being aware of your overall spending. Many people insist that once they began tracking their spending, they started spending less and saving more.

Recording cash spent is important. Every time you write a check for cash or use the automated teller machine (ATM), write down where you actually spend that cash. Itemizing all the cash provides more valuable information for you than just recording "$50 cash" or "misc." six times as an expense and not really knowing how it was spent or "where the money went."

Debit cards and ATMs as conveniences can be either a blessing or a curse depending how you use them. After months of total chaos and overdraft charges in the checking account, one couple worked out their monthly budget to determine exactly how much cash was needed each week. On Mondays Joe gets his lump cash and knows it has to cover his gas, big gulps, meals, snacks, and all other incidentals for the week. Ginny sticks with the checkbook. Both are relieved to always know their current balance in the checkbook.

If you seem to have more month than money most of the time, remember your choices. You can reduce, postpone, modify or eliminate your spending. If you are not sure where to begin, a review of these filled-out worksheets will quickly show you which optional categories to begin with. Maybe you need to do more of your own home or car repairs, be more energy-conscious, eat out less, cut back on gifts, or start car pooling or whatever fits your abilities and interests. When you do cut back, the results will be noticed immediately.

As you work with these worksheets, modify them to fit your unique lifestyle. The expense categories, net income, savings, investment, and retirement sections are all provided as guidelines to set up your own system.

If you have tax-deductible expenses, note them here. If you want all your tax records kept together, you can use the handy **Tax-Deductible Expense Record** in Part Three.

You will notice the emphasis on net income, not on gross income, throughout this workbook. The idea is to deal only with actual money and not record more information than you need to. The gross income information is usually on your check stubs. If you need to keep a record of your taxes, FICA, retirement savings, and other deductions, you can use the "End-of-the-Year Tax Information" section on the bottom of the Summary-for-the-Year worksheet.

Monthly Expense Record

Balance Forward from Last Month:

Cash __$37.00__   Checking __$62.00__   Savings __$11,796.45__

NET INCOME

SALARY/COMMISSIONS	Chris	Kim	TOTAL
	896.00		
		1,407.43	
	883.00		
		1,407.43	
TOTAL INCOME			4,593.86
OTHER			
Yard sale — 273			273.00
TOTAL INCOME			4,866.86

SAVINGS

(Describe)	
Reserve (used other $257 this month)	750.00
Goals	75.00
Emergency	215.00
TOTAL SAVINGS	1,040.00

INVESTMENTS/RETIREMENT

(See Payroll Deduction)	
TOTAL INVESTMENTS	

		FOOD		HOUSEHOLD				TRANSPORTATION			PERSONAL		MEDICAL	
		groceries	meals out school lunches	snacks beverages	mainten. house yard pool	appliance furniture furnishings supplies	misc. postage copies bank chg. film	interest taxes	gas	auto mainten. wash license	transit tolls parking	clothing sewing cleaning shoe care	toiletries cosmetics hair nails massage	doctor dentist medicine vitamins	personal growth therapy
WEEK 1	1	40.00	15.00						13.92						
	2		7.50		20.34	33.67									
	3	5.94							9.35				25.00		65.30
	4			15.31						24.73		21.82		10.20	
	5		28.98												
	6			5.10											
	7	44.48		6.05								15.03			
WEEK 2	8													33.68	
	9	67.10	7.50				29.00					43.98			
	10								14.79						
	11	7.25	14.22										19.00		
	12			4.95										13.00	
	13			5.10	14.76					6.95					
	14			6.05											
WEEK 3	15	10.53											21.46		
	16		12.35						10.45			20.80			
	17														
	18	28.55	7.50	5.10											
	19												25.00		
	20	9.57										13.37			
	21					23.00									65.30
WEEK 4	22			11.08					15.65						
	23			10.45											
	24														
	25	149.73													
	26		7.50	4.95					9.35			15.41			
	27						8.50								
	28	19.52													
	29				4.31										
	30	67.10	27.34						19.95						
	31	8.59													
Total		458.36	127.89	63.69	49.86	56.67	37.50	—	93.46	31.68	—	130.41	90.46	56.88	130.60

 **Monthly Expense Record**

SAMPLE

FIXED EXPENSES

Monthly	Amount	Monthly	Amount
Mortgage/Rent	784.00	Insurance:	
Asso. Fee		House/Apt	
Gas/Fuel	73.00	Auto	
Electricity	89.00	Life	54.00
Water/Refuse		Health (Payroll ded.)	
Garbage/Sewer		Dental	
Telephone	53.21	Disability	
Cellular Phone			
Cable	35.00	Storage	75
Child Support			
Spousal Support			
TOTAL	**1,034.21**	**TOTAL**	**129.00**

INSTALLMENT EXPENSES

Loans/Credit Cards	Amount
Visa	75.00
MC	50.00
Student Loan	167.00
Car Payment	291.00
TOTAL	**583.00**

TOTAL EXPENSES

Total Fixed Expenses	1,163.21
Total Installment Expenses	583.00
Total Monthly Expenses from Below	1,932.05
GRAND TOTAL	**3,678.26**

+ Savings (1040.00) = $4,718.26

RECREATION EDUCATION CHILDREN GENERAL

	vacation trips	entertain. video computer tapes, CDs	sports hobbies lessons clubs	workshop tuition supplies	books magazines software	childcare sitter	allowance toys school expense	pet vet supplies	gifts cards flowers	charitable contribut. church	work expense dues	prof. services lawyer CPA	other (explanation)
1							10.00			50.00			
2		3.21							40.00				
3													
4													
5							10.00						
6													
7										50.00			
8							3.57						
9			19.22										
10									3.59				
11					15.22								
12							10.00						
13										50.00			
14									10.56				
15							15.98						
16													
17		15.04											
18					23.78		10.00						
19									2.60	50.00			
20													
21													
22					39.00								
23							4.98						
24													
25										40.00			
26													
27							10.00						
28		57.84											
29													
30													
31										60.00			
Total	—	76.09	19.22	—	78.00	—	74.53	—	56.75	300.00	—	—	—

Monthly Expense Record

Balance Forward from Last Month:

Cash _____ Checking _____ Savings _____

NET INCOME

			TOTAL
SALARY/COMMISSIONS			
		TOTAL INCOME	
OTHER			
		TOTAL INCOME	

SAVINGS

(Describe)	
	TOTAL SAVINGS

INVESTMENTS/RETIREMENT

	TOTAL INVESTMENTS

	FOOD			HOUSEHOLD					TRANSPORTATION			PERSONAL		MEDICAL	
groceries	meals out school lunches	snacks beverages	mainten. house yard pool	appliance furniture furnishings supplies	misc. postage copies bank chg. film	interest taxes		gas	auto mainten. wash license	transit tolls parking	clothing sewing cleaning shoe care	toiletries cosmetics hair nails massage	doctor dentist medicine vitamins	personal growth therapy
WEEK 1 1															
2															
3															
4															
5															
6															
7															
WEEK 2 8															
9															
10															
11															
12															
13															
14															
WEEK 3 15															
16															
17															
18															
19															
20															
21															
WEEK 4 22															
23															
24															
25															
26															
27															
28															
29															
30															
31															
Total															

Monthly Expense Record

FIXED EXPENSES

Monthly	Amount	Monthly	Amount
Mortgage/Rent		Insurance:	
Asso. Fee		House/Apt	
Gas/Fuel		Auto	
Electricity		Life	
Water/Refuse		Health	
Garbage/Sewer		Dental	
Telephone		Disability	
Cellular Phone			
Cable			
Child Support			
Spousal Support			
TOTAL		**TOTAL**	

INSTALLMENT EXPENSES

Loans/Credit Cards	Amount
TOTAL	

TOTAL EXPENSES

Total Fixed Expenses	
Total Installment Expenses	
Total Monthly Expenses from Below	
GRAND TOTAL	

RECREATION   EDUCATION   CHILDREN   GENERAL

	vacation trips	entertain. video computer tapes, CDs	sports hobbies lessons clubs	workshop tuition supplies	books magazines software	childcare sitter	allowance toys school expense	pet vet supplies	gifts cards flowers	charitable contribut. church	work expense dues	prof. services lawyer CPA	other (explanation)
1													
2													
3													
4													
5													
6													
7													
8													
9													
10													
11													
12													
13													
14													
15													
16													
17													
18													
19													
20													
21													
22													
23													
24													
25													
26													
27													
28													
29													
30													
31													
Total													

Monthly Expense Record

Balance Forward from Last Month:

Cash _____ Checking _____ Savings _____

NET INCOME

			TOTAL
SALARY/COMMISSIONS			
TOTAL INCOME			
OTHER			
TOTAL INCOME			

SAVINGS

(Describe)	
TOTAL SAVINGS	

INVESTMENTS/RETIREMENT

TOTAL INVESTMENTS	

	FOOD			HOUSEHOLD					TRANSPORTATION			PERSONAL		MEDICAL	
	groceries	meals out school lunches	snacks beverages	mainten. house yard pool	appliance furniture furnishings supplies	misc. postage copies bank chg. film	interest taxes		gas	auto mainten. wash license	transit tolls parking	clothing sewing cleaning shoe care	toiletries cosmetics hair nails massage	doctor dentist medicine vitamins	personal growth therapy
WEEK 1 — 1															
2															
3															
4															
5															
6															
7															
WEEK 2 — 8															
9															
10															
11															
12															
13															
14															
WEEK 3 — 15															
16															
17															
18															
19															
20															
21															
WEEK 4 — 22															
23															
24															
25															
26															
27															
28															
29															
30															
31															
Total															

FIXED EXPENSES

Monthly	Amount	Monthly	Amount
Mortgage/Rent		Insurance:	
Asso. Fee		House/Apt	
Gas/Fuel		Auto	
Electricity		Life	
Water/Refuse		Health	
Garbage/Sewer		Dental	
Telephone		Disability	
Cellular Phone			
Cable			
Child Support			
Spousal Support			
TOTAL		**TOTAL**	

INSTALLMENT EXPENSES

Loans/Credit Cards	Amount
TOTAL	

TOTAL EXPENSES

Total Fixed Expenses	
Total Installment Expenses	
Total Monthly Expenses from Below	
GRAND TOTAL	

RECREATION   EDUCATION   CHILDREN   GENERAL

	vacation trips	entertain. video computer tapes, CDs	sports hobbies lessons clubs	workshop tuition supplies	books magazines software	childcare sitter	allowance toys school expense	pet vet supplies	gifts cards flowers	charitable contribut. church	work expense dues	prof. services lawyer CPA	other (explanation)
1													
2													
3													
4													
5													
6													
7													
8													
9													
10													
11													
12													
13													
14													
15													
16													
17													
18													
19													
20													
21													
22													
23													
24													
25													
26													
27													
28													
29													
30													
31													
Total													

Monthly Expense Record

Balance Forward from Last Month:

Cash _____ Checking _____ Savings _____

NET INCOME

			TOTAL
SALARY/COMMISSIONS			
		TOTAL INCOME	
OTHER			
		TOTAL INCOME	

SAVINGS

(Describe)	
	TOTAL SAVINGS	

INVESTMENTS/RETIREMENT

	TOTAL INVESTMENTS	

	FOOD			HOUSEHOLD				TRANSPORTATION			PERSONAL		MEDICAL	
groceries	meals out school lunches	snacks beverages	mainten. house yard pool	appliance furniture furnishings supplies	misc. postage copies bank chg. film	interest taxes		gas	auto mainten. wash license	transit tolls parking	clothing sewing cleaning shoe care	toiletries cosmetics hair nails massage	doctor dentist medicine vitamins	personal growth therapy
WEEK 1 1														
2														
3														
4														
5														
6														
7														
WEEK 2 8														
9														
10														
11														
12														
13														
14														
WEEK 3 15														
16														
17														
18														
19														
20														
21														
WEEK 4 22														
23														
24														
25														
26														
27														
28														
29														
30														
31														
Total														

 **Monthly Expense Record**

FIXED EXPENSES

Monthly	Amount	Monthly	Amount
Mortgage/Rent		Insurance:	
Asso. Fee		House/Apt	
Gas/Fuel		Auto	
Electricity		Life	
Water/Refuse		Health	
Garbage/Sewer		Dental	
Telephone		Disability	
Cellular Phone			
Cable			
Child Support			
Spousal Support			
TOTAL		**TOTAL**	

INSTALLMENT EXPENSES

Loans/Credit Cards	Amount
TOTAL	

TOTAL EXPENSES

Total Fixed Expenses	
Total Installment Expenses	
Total Monthly Expenses from Below	
GRAND TOTAL	

RECREATION   EDUCATION   CHILDREN   GENERAL

	vacation trips	entertain. video computer tapes, CDs	sports hobbies lessons clubs	workshop tuition supplies	books magazines software	childcare sitter	allowance toys school expense	pet vet supplies	gifts cards flowers	charitable contribut. church	work expense dues	prof. services lawyer CPA	other (explanation)
1													
2													
3													
4													
5													
6													
7													
8													
9													
10													
11													
12													
13													
14													
15													
16													
17													
18													
19													
20													
21													
22													
23													
24													
25													
26													
27													
28													
29													
30													
31													
Total													

*M*onthly Expense Record

Balance Forward from Last Month:

Cash _____ Checking _____ Savings _____

NET INCOME

			TOTAL
SALARY/COMMISSIONS			
		TOTAL INCOME	
OTHER			
		TOTAL INCOME	

SAVINGS

(Describe)	
	TOTAL SAVINGS

INVESTMENTS/RETIREMENT

	TOTAL INVESTMENTS

	FOOD			HOUSEHOLD					TRANSPORTATION			PERSONAL		MEDICAL	
	groceries	meals out school lunches	snacks beverages	mainten. house yard pool	appliance furniture furnishings supplies	misc. postage copies bank chg. film	interest taxes		gas	auto mainten. wash license	transit tolls parking	clothing sewing cleaning shoe care	toiletries cosmetics hair nails massage	doctor dentist medicine vitamins	personal growth therapy
WEEK 1 1															
2															
3															
4															
5															
6															
7															
WEEK 2 8															
9															
10															
11															
12															
13															
14															
WEEK 3 15															
16															
17															
18															
19															
20															
21															
WEEK 4 22															
23															
24															
25															
26															
27															
28															
29															
30															
31															
Total															

Monthly Expense Record

FIXED EXPENSES

Monthly	Amount	Monthly	Amount
Mortgage/Rent		Insurance:	
Asso. Fee		House/Apt	
Gas/Fuel		Auto	
Electricity		Life	
Water/Refuse		Health	
Garbage/Sewer		Dental	
Telephone		Disability	
Cellular Phone			
Cable			
Child Support			
Spousal Support			
TOTAL		**TOTAL**	

INSTALLMENT EXPENSES

Loans/Credit Cards	Amount
TOTAL	

TOTAL EXPENSES

Total Fixed Expenses	
Total Installment Expenses	
Total Monthly Expenses from Below	
GRAND TOTAL	

RECREATION EDUCATION CHILDREN GENERAL

	vacation trips	entertain. video computer tapes, CDs	sports hobbies lessons clubs	workshop tuition supplies	books magazines software	childcare sitter	allowance toys school expense	pet vet supplies	gifts cards flowers	charitable contribut. church	work expense dues	prof. services lawyer CPA	other (explanation)
1													
2													
3													
4													
5													
6													
7													
8													
9													
10													
11													
12													
13													
14													
15													
16													
17													
18													
19													
20													
21													
22													
23													
24													
25													
26													
27													
28													
29													
30													
31													
Total													

Monthly Expense Record

Balance Forward from Last Month:

Cash _____ Checking _____ Savings _____

NET INCOME

				TOTAL
SALARY/COMMISSIONS				
		TOTAL INCOME		
OTHER				
		TOTAL INCOME		

SAVINGS

(Describe)	
TOTAL SAVINGS	

INVESTMENTS/RETIREMENT

TOTAL INVESTMENTS	

	FOOD			HOUSEHOLD				TRANSPORTATION			PERSONAL		MEDICAL	
	groceries	meals out school lunches	snacks beverages	mainten. house yard pool	appliance furniture furnishings supplies	misc. postage copies bank chg. film	interest taxes	gas	auto mainten. wash license	transit tolls parking	clothing sewing cleaning shoe care	toiletries cosmetics hair nails massage	doctor dentist medicine vitamins	personal growth therapy
WEEK 1 — 1														
2														
3														
4														
5														
6														
7														
WEEK 2 — 8														
9														
10														
11														
12														
13														
14														
WEEK 3 — 15														
16														
17														
18														
19														
20														
21														
WEEK 4 — 22														
23														
24														
25														
26														
27														
28														
29														
30														
31														
Total														

FIXED EXPENSES

Monthly	Amount	Monthly	Amount
Mortgage/Rent		Insurance:	
Asso. Fee		House/Apt	
Gas/Fuel		Auto	
Electricity		Life	
Water/Refuse		Health	
Garbage/Sewer		Dental	
Telephone		Disability	
Cellular Phone			
Cable			
Child Support			
Spousal Support			
TOTAL		**TOTAL**	

INSTALLMENT EXPENSES

Loans/Credit Cards	Amount
TOTAL	

TOTAL EXPENSES

Total Fixed Expenses	
Total Installment Expenses	
Total Monthly Expenses from Below	
GRAND TOTAL	

	RECREATION		EDUCATION	CHILDREN			GENERAL					
vacation trips	entertain. video computer tapes, CDs	sports hobbies lessons clubs	workshop tuition supplies	books magazines software	childcare sitter	allowance toys school expense	pet vet supplies	gifts cards flowers	charitable contribut. church	work expense dues	prof. services lawyer CPA	other (explanation)
1												
2												
3												
4												
5												
6												
7												
8												
9												
10												
11												
12												
13												
14												
15												
16												
17												
18												
19												
20												
21												
22												
23												
24												
25												
26												
27												
28												
29												
30												
31												
Total												

Monthly Expense Record

Balance Forward from Last Month:

Cash _____ Checking _____ Savings _____

NET INCOME

			TOTAL
SALARY/COMMISSIONS			
		TOTAL INCOME	
OTHER			
		TOTAL INCOME	

SAVINGS

(Describe)	
TOTAL SAVINGS	

INVESTMENTS/RETIREMENT

TOTAL INVESTMENTS	

	FOOD			HOUSEHOLD			TRANSPORTATION				PERSONAL		MEDICAL	
	groceries	meals out school lunches	snacks beverages	mainten. house yard pool	appliance furniture furnishings supplies	misc. postage copies bank chg. film	interest taxes	gas	auto mainten. wash license	transit tolls parking	clothing sewing cleaning shoe care	toiletries cosmetics hair nails massage	doctor dentist medicine vitamins	personal growth therapy
WEEK 1 — 1														
2														
3														
4														
5														
6														
7														
WEEK 2 — 8														
9														
10														
11														
12														
13														
14														
WEEK 3 — 15														
16														
17														
18														
19														
20														
21														
WEEK 4 — 22														
23														
24														
25														
26														
27														
28														
29														
30														
31														
Total														

Monthly Expense Record

FIXED EXPENSES

Monthly	Amount	Monthly	Amount
Mortgage/Rent		Insurance:	
Asso. Fee		House/Apt	
Gas/Fuel		Auto	
Electricity		Life	
Water/Refuse		Health	
Garbage/Sewer		Dental	
Telephone		Disability	
Cellular Phone			
Cable			
Child Support			
Spousal Support			
TOTAL		**TOTAL**	

INSTALLMENT EXPENSES

Loans/Credit Cards	Amount
TOTAL	

TOTAL EXPENSES

Total Fixed Expenses	
Total Installment Expenses	
Total Monthly Expenses from Below	
GRAND TOTAL	

RECREATION   EDUCATION   CHILDREN   GENERAL

	vacation trips	entertain. video computer tapes, CDs	sports hobbies lessons clubs	workshop tuition supplies	books magazines software	childcare sitter	allowance toys school expense	pet vet supplies	gifts cards flowers	charitable contribut. church	work expense dues	prof. services lawyer CPA	other (explanation)
1													
2													
3													
4													
5													
6													
7													
8													
9													
10													
11													
12													
13													
14													
15													
16													
17													
18													
19													
20													
21													
22													
23													
24													
25													
26													
27													
28													
29													
30													
31													
Total													

Monthly Expense Record

Balance Forward from Last Month:

Cash _____ Checking _____ Savings _____

NET INCOME

			TOTAL
SALARY/COMMISSIONS			
	TOTAL INCOME		
OTHER			
	TOTAL INCOME		

SAVINGS

(Describe)	
TOTAL SAVINGS	

INVESTMENTS/RETIREMENT

TOTAL INVESTMENTS	

	FOOD			HOUSEHOLD					TRANSPORTATION			PERSONAL		MEDICAL	
	groceries	meals out school lunches	snacks beverages	mainten. house yard pool	appliance furniture furnishings supplies	misc. postage copies bank chg. film	interest taxes		gas	auto mainten. wash license	transit tolls parking	clothing sewing cleaning shoe care	toiletries cosmetics hair nails massage	doctor dentist medicine vitamins	personal growth therapy
WEEK 1 — 1															
2															
3															
4															
5															
6															
7															
WEEK 2 — 8															
9															
10															
11															
12															
13															
14															
WEEK 3 — 15															
16															
17															
18															
19															
20															
21															
WEEK 4 — 22															
23															
24															
25															
26															
27															
28															
29															
30															
31															
Total															

FIXED EXPENSES

Monthly	Amount	Monthly	Amount
Mortgage/Rent		Insurance:	
Asso. Fee		House/Apt	
Gas/Fuel		Auto	
Electricity		Life	
Water/Refuse		Health	
Garbage/Sewer		Dental	
Telephone		Disability	
Cellular Phone			
Cable			
Child Support			
Spousal Support			
TOTAL		**TOTAL**	

INSTALLMENT EXPENSES

Loans/Credit Cards	Amount
TOTAL	

TOTAL EXPENSES

Total Fixed Expenses	
Total Installment Expenses	
Total Monthly Expenses from Below	
GRAND TOTAL	

RECREATION   EDUCATION   CHILDREN   GENERAL

	vacation trips	entertain. video computer tapes, CDs	sports hobbies lessons clubs	workshop tuition supplies	books magazines software	childcare sitter	allowance toys school expense	pet vet supplies	gifts cards flowers	charitable contribut. church	work expense dues	prof. services lawyer CPA	other (explanation)
1													
2													
3													
4													
5													
6													
7													
8													
9													
10													
11													
12													
13													
14													
15													
16													
17													
18													
19													
20													
21													
22													
23													
24													
25													
26													
27													
28													
29													
30													
31													
Total													

Monthly Expense Record

Balance Forward from Last Month:
Cash _____ Checking _____ Savings _____

NET INCOME

			TOTAL
SALARY/COMMISSIONS			
		TOTAL INCOME	
OTHER			
		TOTAL INCOME	

SAVINGS

(Describe)	
TOTAL SAVINGS	

INVESTMENTS/RETIREMENT

TOTAL INVESTMENTS	

	FOOD			HOUSEHOLD				TRANSPORTATION			PERSONAL		MEDICAL	
	groceries	meals out school lunches	snacks beverages	mainten. house yard pool	appliance furniture furnishings supplies	misc. postage copies bank chg. film	interest taxes	gas	auto mainten. wash license	transit tolls parking	clothing sewing cleaning shoe care	toiletries cosmetics hair nails massage	doctor dentist medicine vitamins	personal growth therapy
WEEK 1 1														
2														
3														
4														
5														
6														
7														
WEEK 2 8														
9														
10														
11														
12														
13														
14														
WEEK 3 15														
16														
17														
18														
19														
20														
21														
WEEK 4 22														
23														
24														
25														
26														
27														
28														
29														
30														
31														
Total														

FIXED EXPENSES

Monthly	Amount	Monthly	Amount
Mortgage/Rent		Insurance:	
Asso. Fee		House/Apt	
Gas/Fuel		Auto	
Electricity		Life	
Water/Refuse		Health	
Garbage/Sewer		Dental	
Telephone		Disability	
Cellular Phone			
Cable			
Child Support			
Spousal Support			
TOTAL		**TOTAL**	

INSTALLMENT EXPENSES

Loans/Credit Cards	Amount
TOTAL	

TOTAL EXPENSES

Total Fixed Expenses	
Total Installment Expenses	
Total Monthly Expenses from Below	
GRAND TOTAL	

	RECREATION		EDUCATION	CHILDREN			GENERAL					
	vacation trips	entertain. video computer tapes, CDs	sports hobbies lessons clubs	workshop tuition supplies	books magazines software	childcare sitter	allowance toys school expense	pet vet supplies	gifts cards flowers	charitable contribut. church	work expense dues	prof. services lawyer CPA	other (explanation)
1													
2													
3													
4													
5													
6													
7													
8													
9													
10													
11													
12													
13													
14													
15													
16													
17													
18													
19													
20													
21													
22													
23													
24													
25													
26													
27													
28													
29													
30													
31													
Total													

Monthly Expense Record

Balance Forward from Last Month:

Cash _____ Checking _____ Savings _____

NET INCOME

			TOTAL
SALARY/COMMISSIONS			
		TOTAL INCOME	
OTHER			
		TOTAL INCOME	

SAVINGS

(Describe)	
TOTAL SAVINGS	

INVESTMENTS/RETIREMENT

TOTAL INVESTMENTS	

	FOOD			HOUSEHOLD			TRANSPORTATION				PERSONAL		MEDICAL	
	groceries	meals out school lunches	snacks beverages	mainten. house yard pool	appliance furniture furnishings supplies	misc. postage copies bank chg. film	interest taxes	gas	auto mainten. wash license	transit tolls parking	clothing sewing cleaning shoe care	toiletries cosmetics hair nails massage	doctor dentist medicine vitamins	personal growth therapy
WEEK 1 — 1														
2														
3														
4														
5														
6														
7														
WEEK 2 — 8														
9														
10														
11														
12														
13														
14														
WEEK 3 — 15														
16														
17														
18														
19														
20														
21														
WEEK 4 — 22														
23														
24														
25														
26														
27														
28														
29														
30														
31														
Total														

FIXED EXPENSES

Monthly	Amount	Monthly	Amount
Mortgage/Rent		Insurance:	
Asso. Fee		House/Apt	
Gas/Fuel		Auto	
Electricity		Life	
Water/Refuse		Health	
Garbage/Sewer		Dental	
Telephone		Disability	
Cellular Phone			
Cable			
Child Support			
Spousal Support			
TOTAL		**TOTAL**	

INSTALLMENT EXPENSES

Loans/Credit Cards	Amount
TOTAL	

TOTAL EXPENSES

Total Fixed Expenses	
Total Installment Expenses	
Total Monthly Expenses from Below	
GRAND TOTAL	

RECREATION   EDUCATION CHILDREN   GENERAL

	vacation trips	entertain. video computer tapes, CDs	sports hobbies lessons clubs	workshop tuition supplies	books magazines software	childcare sitter	allowance toys school expense	pet vet supplies	gifts cards flowers	charitable contribut. church	work expense dues	prof. services lawyer CPA	other (explanation)
1													
2													
3													
4													
5													
6													
7													
8													
9													
10													
11													
12													
13													
14													
15													
16													
17													
18													
19													
20													
21													
22													
23													
24													
25													
26													
27													
28													
29													
30													
31													
Total													

Monthly Expense Record

Balance Forward from Last Month:

Cash _____ Checking _____ Savings _____

NET INCOME

			TOTAL
SALARY/COMMISSIONS			
		TOTAL INCOME	
OTHER			
		TOTAL INCOME	

SAVINGS

(Describe)	
	TOTAL SAVINGS	

INVESTMENTS/RETIREMENT

TOTAL INVESTMENTS	

	FOOD			HOUSEHOLD					TRANSPORTATION			PERSONAL		MEDICAL	
	groceries	meals out school lunches	snacks beverages	mainten. house yard pool	appliance furniture furnishings supplies	misc. postage copies bank chg. film	interest taxes		gas	auto mainten. wash license	transit tolls parking	clothing sewing cleaning shoe care	toiletries cosmetics hair nails massage	doctor dentist medicine vitamins	personal growth therapy
WEEK 1 — 1															
2															
3															
4															
5															
6															
7															
WEEK 2 — 8															
9															
10															
11															
12															
13															
14															
WEEK 3 — 15															
16															
17															
18															
19															
20															
21															
WEEK 4 — 22															
23															
24															
25															
26															
27															
28															
29															
30															
31															
Total															

 onthly Expense Record

FIXED EXPENSES

Monthly	Amount	Monthly	Amount
Mortgage/Rent		Insurance:	
Asso. Fee		House/Apt	
Gas/Fuel		Auto	
Electricity		Life	
Water/Refuse		Health	
Garbage/Sewer		Dental	
Telephone		Disability	
Cellular Phone			
Cable			
Child Support			
Spousal Support			
TOTAL		**TOTAL**	

INSTALLMENT EXPENSES

Loans/Credit Cards	Amount
TOTAL	

TOTAL EXPENSES

Total Fixed Expenses	
Total Installment Expenses	
Total Monthly Expenses from Below	
GRAND TOTAL	

RECREATION   EDUCATION   CHILDREN   GENERAL

	vacation trips	entertain. video computer tapes, CDs	sports hobbies lessons clubs	workshop tuition supplies	books magazines software	childcare sitter	allowance toys school expense	pet vet supplies	gifts cards flowers	charitable contribut. church	work expense dues	prof. services lawyer CPA	other (explanation)
1													
2													
3													
4													
5													
6													
7													
8													
9													
10													
11													
12													
13													
14													
15													
16													
17													
18													
19													
20													
21													
22													
23													
24													
25													
26													
27													
28													
29													
30													
31													
Total													

Monthly Expense Record

Balance Forward from Last Month:

Cash _____ Checking _____ Savings _____

NET INCOME

			TOTAL
SALARY/COMMISSIONS			
	TOTAL INCOME		
OTHER			
	TOTAL INCOME		

SAVINGS

(Describe)	
	TOTAL SAVINGS

INVESTMENTS/RETIREMENT

	TOTAL INVESTMENTS

	FOOD			HOUSEHOLD					TRANSPORTATION				PERSONAL		MEDICAL	
	groceries	meals out school lunches	snacks beverages	mainten. house yard pool	appliance furniture furnishings supplies	misc. postage copies bank chg. film	interest taxes		gas	auto mainten. wash license	transit tolls parking	clothing sewing cleaning shoe care	toiletries cosmetics hair nails massage	doctor dentist medicine vitamins	personal growth therapy
WEEK 1 1															
2															
3															
4															
5															
6															
7															
WEEK 2 8															
9															
10															
11															
12															
13															
14															
WEEK 3 15															
16															
17															
18															
19															
20															
21															
WEEK 4 22															
23															
24															
25															
26															
27															
28															
29															
30															
31															
Total															

FIXED EXPENSES

Monthly	Amount	Monthly	Amount
Mortgage/Rent		Insurance:	
Asso. Fee		House/Apt	
Gas/Fuel		Auto	
Electricity		Life	
Water/Refuse		Health	
Garbage/Sewer		Dental	
Telephone		Disability	
Cellular Phone			
Cable			
Child Support			
Spousal Support			
TOTAL		**TOTAL**	

INSTALLMENT EXPENSES

Loans/Credit Cards	Amount
TOTAL	

TOTAL EXPENSES

Total Fixed Expenses	
Total Installment Expenses	
Total Monthly Expenses from Below	
GRAND TOTAL	

RECREATION EDUCATION CHILDREN GENERAL

	vacation trips	entertain. video computer tapes, CDs	sports hobbies lessons clubs	workshop tuition supplies	books magazines software	childcare sitter	allowance toys school expense	pet vet supplies	gifts cards flowers	charitable contribut. church	work expense dues	prof. services lawyer CPA	other (explanation)
1													
2													
3													
4													
5													
6													
7													
8													
9													
10													
11													
12													
13													
14													
15													
16													
17													
18													
19													
20													
21													
22													
23													
24													
25													
26													
27													
28													
29													
30													
31													
Total													

Monthly Expense Record

Balance Forward from Last Month:

Cash _____ Checking _____ Savings _____

NET INCOME			TOTAL
SALARY/COMMISSIONS			
		TOTAL INCOME	
OTHER			
		TOTAL INCOME	

SAVINGS	
(Describe)	
	TOTAL SAVINGS	

INVESTMENTS/RETIREMENT	
	TOTAL INVESTMENTS	

	FOOD			HOUSEHOLD					TRANSPORTATION			PERSONAL		MEDICAL	
	groceries	meals out school lunches	snacks beverages	mainten. house yard pool	appliance furniture furnishings supplies	misc. postage copies bank chg. film	interest taxes		gas	auto mainten. wash license	transit tolls parking	clothing sewing cleaning shoe care	toiletries cosmetics hair nails massage	doctor dentist medicine vitamins	personal growth therapy
WEEK 1 1															
2															
3															
4															
5															
6															
7															
WEEK 2 8															
9															
10															
11															
12															
13															
14															
WEEK 3 15															
16															
17															
18															
19															
20															
21															
WEEK 4 22															
23															
24															
25															
26															
27															
28															
29															
30															
31															
Total															

Monthly Expense Record

FIXED EXPENSES

Monthly	Amount	Monthly	Amount
Mortgage/Rent		Insurance:	
Asso. Fee		House/Apt	
Gas/Fuel		Auto	
Electricity		Life	
Water/Refuse		Health	
Garbage/Sewer		Dental	
Telephone		Disability	
Cellular Phone			
Cable			
Child Support			
Spousal Support			
TOTAL		**TOTAL**	

INSTALLMENT EXPENSES

Loans/Credit Cards	Amount
TOTAL	

TOTAL EXPENSES

Total Fixed Expenses	
Total Installment Expenses	
Total Monthly Expenses from Below	
GRAND TOTAL	

	RECREATION		EDUCATION	CHILDREN			GENERAL					
	vacation trips	entertain. video computer tapes, CDs	sports hobbies lessons clubs	workshop tuition supplies	books magazines software	childcare sitter	allowance toys school expense	pet vet supplies	gifts cards flowers	charitable contribut. church	work expense dues	prof. services lawyer CPA	other (explanation)
1													
2													
3													
4													
5													
6													
7													
8													
9													
10													
11													
12													
13													
14													
15													
16													
17													
18													
19													
20													
21													
22													
23													
24													
25													
26													
27													
28													
29													
30													
31													
Total													

Summary-for-the-Year Record/
End-of-the-Year Tax Information

The totals you have at the end of each month in the Monthly Expense Record Worksheet can be transferred to this section so you will have a total picture and a way to compare monthly expenses for each category.

This Summary-for-the-Year Record is excellent for measuring your financial progress and setting your future goals.

Summary-for-the-Year Record

		JAN.	FEB.	MAR.	APR.	MAY	JUNE	JULY	AUG.	SEPT.	OCT.	NOV.	DEC.	Total	Mo. Avg.
Net Income	Salary/ Commission														
	Other														
Food	Groceries														
	School Lunches Meals Out														
	Snacks Beverages														
Household	Supplies, Maintenance, House, Yard, Pool														
	Appliance, Furniture, Furnishings, Supplies														
	Postage, Copies, Bank Charges, Film, Miscellaneous														
	Interest, Taxes														
Transportation	Gas														
	Automobile Maintenance, Wash, License														
	Transit, Tolls, Parking														
Personal	Clothing, Sewing, Cleaning, Shoe Care														
	Cosmetics, Hair, Nails, Massage, Toiletries														
Medical	Doctor, Dentist, Medicine, Vitamins														
	Personal Growth Therapy														
Recreation	Vacation, Trips														
	Entertain., Video, Computer, Tapes, CDs														
	Sports, Hobbies, Lessons, Clubs														

Summary for Monthly Savings/Investments/Retirement

	JAN.	FEB.	MAR.	APR.	MAY	JUNE	JULY	AUG.	SEPT.	OCT.	NOV.	DEC.	Total
Savings													
Investments													
Retirement													
Total													

		JAN.	FEB.	MAR.	APR.	MAY	JUNE	JULY	AUG.	SEPT.	OCT.	NOV.	DEC.	Total	Mo. Avg.
Education	Tuition, Supplies Workshop														
Education	Books, Magazines, Software														
Children	Child Care, Sitter														
Children	Allowance, Toys, School Expense														
General	Pet, Vet, Supplies														
General	Gifts, Cards, Flowers														
General	Charitable Contribut., Church														
General	Work Expense, Dues														
General	Prof. Serv., Lawyer, CPA														
General	Other														
Home	Mortgage, Rent, Assn. Fees														
Utilities	Gas, Electric														
Utilities	Water, Garbage														
Utilities	Phone, Cable														
Support	Child, Spousal														
Insurance	Home, Auto, Life, Health, Disability														
Installment	Loans, Credit Cards														
Total	Monthly Expenses														

End-of-the-Year Tax Information

	JAN.	FEB.	MAR.	APR.	MAY	JUNE	JULY	AUG.	SEPT.	OCT.	NOV.	DEC.	Total
Federal													
State													
FICA													
Other Deductions													
Total													

Part Three

Medical Expense Record

Tax-Deductible Expense Record

Miscellaneous Expense Record

Investment/Savings Record

Child Support Records

Subscription Record

Mail Order Purchase Record

This collection of worksheets for keeping records and recording expenses will help you keep your financial records organized. Look through each of these forms to see which worksheets apply to you and will be helpful for your particular household's financial situation.

Medical Expense Record

If you need to keep additional records on medical expenses, use these worksheets. The first page, Doctor, Dentist, and Hospital Visits, can be used for recording all visits including nontraditional health care. Include the costs here whether they are full pay, co-pay, or are going to be reimbursed by insurance. If you have a lot of prescription, lab tests, and other related medical expenses (like glasses, crutches, rental medical equipment, etc.) then use the second page, Medical Expenses, Prescriptions, and Other to keep those expense records separate.

Again, these worksheets are a guideline so adjust them to work for your medical recordkeeping needs.

A space is provided for mileage, which at this writing is tax-deductible. The columns for "Date Submitted" and "Insurance Reimbursements" is provided for those households paying the medical bills first before submitting claims or paying the differences not covered by insurance and wanting to keep this information separate.

During tax time this information will save you hours of preparation time.

Medical Expense Record

DOCTOR, DENTIST AND HOSPITAL VISITS

Date	Mileage	To Whom Paid	Amount	Date Submitted	Insurance Reimbursements Amount/Date Paid
		Total			
		Total Amount Paid			
		Total Reimbursed			
		Total Medical Cost			

MEDICAL EXPENSES, PRESCRIPTIONS AND OTHER

Date	Mileage	To Whom Paid	Amount	Date Submitted	Insurance Reimbursements Amount/Date Paid
		Total			
		Total Amount Paid			
		Total Reimbursed			
		Total Medical Cost			

Tax-Deductible Expense Record

After you record your expenses on the **Monthly Expense Record** worksheets, take a moment to jot down deductible expenses on the Tax-Deductible Expense Record so you have all your deductible expenses recorded in one place. When you prepare next year's tax return, itemizing deductions will be a very quick and efficient process.

Each year, tax deductions may vary. This worksheet is designed to be a convenient record of all deductions applying to your circumstances and the current tax laws. Include categories such as education, professional or union dues, child care, alimony, casualty losses, etc. If you have regular or multiple deductions in one category, the Multiple Tax-Deductible Expenses Record may be more convenient for recording those records.

Consult your tax professional regarding any changes in tax law for these or any other tax-related records.

The IRS audited my records and said they were so good it was no problem and they accepted all of it. My insurance company also accepted my records without having receipts. I'm 68 years old and have used this book for ten years and I'm buying ten more for the next ten years.

Tax-Deductible Expense Record

Date	Description (Donation/Payment To)	Check Number	Amount/Value: Taxes/ Interest	Charitable Contribution	_____	_____
		Total				

Multiple Tax-Deductible Expenses Record

CATEGORY: _____		
Date	Description	Amount
	Total	

CATEGORY: _____		
Date	Description	Amount
	Total	

Miscellaneous Expense Record

A variety of additional generic worksheets are provided for other records such as major household purchases, home improvement projects, car expenses, college costs, etc. Use any of these or the other variety of worksheets in this workbook to best fit your particular needs.

Record of_____   *Miscellaneous Expense Record Year 19____*

	JAN.	FEB.	MAR.	APR.	MAY	JUNE	JULY	AUG.	SEPT.	OCT.	NOV.	DEC.	TOTAL
Total													

Miscellaneous Expense Record

Date	To Whom Paid/Service	Amount		Date	To Whom Paid/Service	Amount
		Total				Total

Investment/Savings Record

YOUR INVESTMENT PICTURE

If you followed the suggestions and guidelines in this workbook, you probably already have or soon will have some basic savings and investments.

Whether you have money in company savings plans, inherited some stocks and bonds, invested in mutual funds, changed your savings from passbooks to certificates of deposit (CDs) or money markets, or opened an Individual Retirement Account (IRA), it is important to keep all your records in one place and know what you have. These records are extremely useful for preparing income tax, completing financial statements, and helping your heirs in the event of an unexpected death.

As with personal finances, if you don't pay attention to your investments or keep careful records of them, you may easily forget what you have or where you have them. Soon it may be hard to remember just exactly where you put those IRAs that you purchased sometime in 1988 and 1991. What rates are they getting? What are the maturity dates?

Or maybe through your parents or a divorce, you acquired some stocks that are just "sitting" in an account and you really don't know what you have. With today's fast-paced lifestyle, it is easy to leave the responsibility of knowing what you own to someone else—a banker, a broker, or an accountant—but by doing so, you sacrifice an understanding and awareness of your total financial picture.

The Investment/Savings Record worksheet provides a place for recording key information about your various investments. The space on the right allows for a periodic follow-up of your current yield. The headings are used as a guideline. If necessary, change them to make them appropriate for your investments.

If you anticipate frequent changes, you should record general information at the beginning of the year here and use the other worksheets in this section of the workbook to record your investment and savings activity. You can modify the **Savings Activity Record, Retirement Savings Record** or **Miscellaneous Expense Record** to fit your needs. The important point is to be sure that you have recorded all the information for each of your investments and have it all in one convenient place.

RESERVE FUNDS

Use this section of the Investment/Saving Record to record information about your liquid-asset accounts (money you have available for immediate use without withdrawal penalties). These include investments in money markets or savings in your bank and/or credit union.

If you have ongoing monthly savings activity, you can use the **Savings Activity Record** worksheet to record your month-to-month transactions. On that page, you can list your savings for upcoming taxes or insurance (reserve account), unexpected car or home repairs (emergency account), or vacation and Christmas savings (goal account).

RETIREMENT

Record the information for your retirement savings programs here. Your monthly savings activity can be recorded on the **Retirement Savings Record** in this section. These programs range from savings funded and/or established by your employer, to personal IRAs, Keoghs, company pensions and other tax-sheltered investments.

A wide variety of employee-retirement programs are offered through schools, hospitals, government and private firms. It is easy to forget or ignore these funds for they often are only shown as paycheck deductions. Pay attention to and gather up the necessary information as outlined in this section so you are familiar with your current and past retirement programs.

SHORT- AND LONG-TERM HOLDINGS

Record your investments held for short or extended periods in the Investment/Savings Record. Some of these investments, such as CDs, T-bills, bonds, etc., will have fixed rates or time periods and this information should be noted on the worksheet. Other securities (stocks, mutual funds, options) may change yields, time frames and prices daily. Because this worksheet has limited space for all the variable information, use this worksheet for beginning- and end-of-the-year summaries.

If you frequently buy, sell and actively get involved with your investments, you already may have an investment portfolio with all the necessary information. On the other hand, if you do not do much with your investments, especially securities, *the information on this worksheet will be extremely helpful for tax, loan, or net-worth purposes.*

OTHER INVESTMENTS

Your investments, such as real estate (other than personal residence), collectibles, trusts, limited or general partnerships, etc., also would be recorded here. If the majority of those other investments are quite extensive, however, you probably have them recorded through another system. If so, indicate where you have those records. The same is true for any of your other investments listed on this worksheet.

MAINTAINING CONTROL OF YOUR FINANCES

As you gather your investment information, you may find you need to develop your own follow-up system for those long-range investments with maturity dates. Start a file and keep a copy of these worksheets for each year. Highlight the maturity dates so you have a quick reference.

While reviewing your investments take time to monitor the returns and determine how well your investments are performing.

These worksheets, along with the others you have used in this workbook, will help you to record all your financial information in one place, thus staying organized and aware of your finances.

Investment/Savings Record

RESERVE FUNDS (Checking, Savings, Money Market, etc.)

Name of Institution	Type	Account Number	Date Opened	Amount Invested	Interest Rate	Owned by (husband, wife, joint)

RETIREMENT ACCOUNTS (IRA, TSA, 401(k), 403(b), SEP, Keogh, etc.)

Where Held	Type and Name	Account Number	Purchase Date	Amount Invested	Interest Rate	Maturity Date

SHORT- AND LONG-TERM HOLDINGS (Mutual Funds, Stocks, Bonds, etc.)

Where Held	Type and Name	Certificate/ Account Number	Purchase Date	Amount Invested	Number of Shares	Unit Price	Dividend/ Interest Rate

OTHER (Real Estate, Collectibles, etc.)

Location/Name	Date Purchased	Cost	Monthly/Yearly Income	Location of Records

Investment/Savings Record

RESERVE FUNDS

Contact Name/Telephone	Location of Records	Follow-Up Information (date, balance, current yield)

RETIREMENT ACCOUNTS

Owned by (husband, wife, joint)	Contact Name/Telephone	Location of Records	Date Sold	Net Proceeds	Gain/Loss	Additional Notes (rollover information)

SHORT- AND LONG-TERM HOLDINGS

Date/Amount Dividend Paid	Maturity Date	Owned By (husband, wife, joint)	Contact Name/Telephone	Location of Records	Date Sold	Number of Shares Sold	Net Proceeds	Gain/Loss

OTHER

Additional Notes (date sold, total proceeds, etc.)

Savings Activity Record

EMERGENCY

Institution: _____   Account Number: _____

	JAN.	FEB.	MAR.	APR.	MAY	JUNE	JULY	AUG.	SEPT.	OCT.	NOV.	DEC.
Deposits												
Withdrawals												
Interest earned												
Balance												

RESERVE

Institution: _____   Account Number: _____

	JAN.	FEB.	MAR.	APR.	MAY	JUNE	JULY	AUG.	SEPT.	OCT.	NOV.	DEC.
Deposits												
Withdrawals												
Interest earned												
Balance												

GOALS/CHRISTMAS

Institution: _____   Account Number: _____

	JAN.	FEB.	MAR.	APR.	MAY	JUNE	JULY	AUG.	SEPT.	OCT.	NOV.	DEC.
Deposits												
Withdrawals												
Interest earned												
Balance												

OTHER

Institution: _____   Account Number: _____

	JAN.	FEB.	MAR.	APR.	MAY	JUNE	JULY	AUG.	SEPT.	OCT.	NOV.	DEC.
Deposits												
Withdrawals												
Interest earned												
Balance												

*R*etirement Savings Record

NAME

Date	Program (IRA, 401(k), etc.): _____ _____			Date	Program (IRA, 401(k), etc.): _____ _____		
Total				Total			

NAME

Date	Program (IRA, 401(k), etc.): _____ _____			Date	Program (IRA, 401(k), etc.): _____ _____		
Total				Total			

Child Support Records

Earlier this year I needed a personal loan. I could not have qualified if I had no proof of child support. The record in this workbook was sufficient information for the bank's approval.

KEEPING RECORDS

After a divorce, it is so easy for depression, anger, fear and loneliness to interfere with practical thoughts and actions.

During this time, credit problems often crop up. This is not because you are incapable of managing your money, but often because you suddenly are overwhelmed with handling all the aspects of family life and household maintenance. Due dates, bills, and paperwork may just seem to get away from you.

Keeping proper records of child support payments, children's expenses, and pertinent custody information is extremely important. However, because of the demands of trying to meet the physical and emotional needs of your children and yourself, these records often are neglected or are never established.

The following worksheets were designed to help remove some of the burden of keeping important records. The worksheets provide guidelines to help you remember what records you should keep and provide you with a tool for having all your necessary information and records in one place. By organizing and controlling this aspect of your life, you will be better equipped to move on to other pressing issues that you face every day.

If you are the noncustodial parent making the child support payments, recording the information called for can be just as important for you. If you must prove what amount and when a support payment actually was made,

received and cashed, or must prove other significant information for tax or legal purposes, you will have the necessary records.

Utilize and modify the worksheets in this book so that you can record information that is unique to your needs. For example, you may want to use the Medical and Dental Expense section of this workbook for keeping detailed records of who paid a medical expense, the insurance deductible or the difference not paid by insurance.

When using these worksheets, be aware that the state and federal laws and regulations vary. *The worksheets and text are not a substitute for legal advice from your local attorney. Consult with your attorney for any questions in this section.*

CHILD SUPPORT PAYMENT RECORD

These records are critical when you need help from your local enforcement agency because of late, short, or missing payments. The "Amount Due" column is for the ① monthly child support payment as ordered. Enter the amount received under *the month* it was due. If no payment was received that month, note that under "Amount ② Received." Because these payments may vary from once a week, or once a month, to sporadically for the year, you will have to modify this column to fit your needs.

Record the other related child support obligations as ③ ordered by the divorce decree, such as medical insurance premium, unreimbursed medical expense, tuition, dues, etc. Also keep records of conversations concerning finances with case workers, ex-spouse, and others. Keep a copy of your decree, stating the terms, payment, custody, visitation, conditions of support, and your record of conversations in a convenient file.

④ Note under "Additional Information" if an item was substituted in lieu of a child support payment. Be sure to check with your attorney if this is an *acceptable form of child support*. If you do not wish to accept an item in lieu of a payment, ask your attorney if written notice should be given. If so, be sure to keep a copy.

⑤ When recording the institution, number and date of the check or money order, use the symbols shown to indicate how the payment was made. If possible, keep a copy of all checks, money orders and envelopes, especially if there is a regular problem with support being on time. These copies will be helpful if a court or social agency ever needs to review your records in the event that there is an excessive lag between the date of the check and the date it was sent, or payment was stopped on a check or money order you received. Be sure to note if you are unable to make a copy of the checks, money orders, or envelopes.

You will find that this worksheet will contain some of your most important records. Stay with it.

THE COST OF RAISING CHILDREN

If you need or want to analyze the cost of raising your children, to show the use of support provided, or to demonstrate the need for increased support, use the **Monthly Expense Record** section.

Enter all your children's daily expenses along with all your other expenses on the Monthly Expense Record pages. Modify the headings to fit your individual needs. Use a highlighter, colored pencil, or check mark to show which expenses are the children's. Total the children's expenses in the columns that apply and record the total at the bottom of the page below the family total. If you have a question about allocating expenses shared by you and your children, ask your local attorney.

Another method used by some families for keeping accurate records is a separate checking account and/or a credit card used strictly for children's expenses. Use the method that works best for you.

If you save all your receipts in envelopes labeled for the different categories, you can file these in your filing system.

CHILD SUPPORT ENFORCEMENT AND CHILD VISITATION RECORDS

In 1984, Congress passed the Child Support Enforcement Amendments of 1984 that strengthen the child support enforcement laws throughout the country. The information you record will be invaluable if you ever need the services of a Child Support Enforcement Bureau in your state to help you collect past-due child support.

If you would like more information about Child Support Enforcement, write the Consumer Information Center, Dept. 633 B, Pueblo, CO 81009, and ask for a free copy of "Kids, They're Worth Every Penny: Handbook on Child Support Enforcement," provided by the Office of Child Support Enforcement in Washington, D.C.

A basic Child Visitation Record is provided if you need a way to record specific dates of visitation each month.

For a more extensive way to keep track of time sharing, holidays, school activities, and other important events being shared between two households, order "My Two Homes—The Divorce Calendar for Kids" ($20.90), LadyBug Press, P.O. Box 7249, Albuquerque, NM 87102-7249, 1-800-244-1761. This is a great calendar which was developed by an attorney. With its design and hundreds of colorful stickers, it gives kids whose parents are divorced a visual and fun way to know their schedules. You can start it any time of the year.

REDUCED ANXIETY

These worksheets cannot take away the pain. They can, however, help reduce some of the anxiety associated with the aftermath of a divorce. As you start taking charge of your situation and gain new knowledge, you will regain self-confidence and self-esteem in the process.

Best of luck to you!

Child Support Payment Record

Balance Due (from previous year) $_____

Month	① Amount Due	② Amount Received	Amount Past Due	⑤ Number on: x—$ Order ✓—Check $—Cash	Date on: x—$ Order ✓—Check $—Cash	Date Payment Received	⑤ Institution and Account Number	③ Other Expenses*	④ Additional Information/ Action Taken (check status, gifts, etc.)
JAN.									
FEB.									
MAR.									
APR.									
MAY									
JUNE									
JULY									
AUG.									
SEPT.									
OCT.									
NOV.									
DEC.									
Total									

*Stipulated by decree

Child Support Enforcement Record

Noncustodial Parent

Full Name

_____

Last-Known Address(es)

_____

_____

_____

Address Dates _____

Home Telephone

_____

Social Security Number

_____

Birth Date/Place _____

_____

Height _____ Weight _____

Occupation

_____

Last Known Employer(s)

_____

_____

Address

_____

_____

_____

_____

Address Dates _____

Work Telephone

_____

Child Support Enforcement Office

Address

_____

_____

_____

Telephone Number

_____

Case Worker's Name/Telephone

_____

_____

Case Number

_____

Court Order Number

_____

Note: Get a Birth Registration Card from your Vital Statistics Office. This will have all your children's information printed on it so you will have the information handy.

Child Visitation Record

DATES OF VISITATION

JAN.	FEB.	MAR.	APR.	MAY	JUNE	JULY	AUG.	SEPT.	OCT.	NOV.	DEC.

Subscription Record

If you ever waited three months to receive your subscription or learned that your magazine gift took that long before it was ever received, you will appreciate having all this information at your fingertips.

Having this record is also an easy way to organize all your subscription amounts and dates due in one central place. You can then transfer this information to the **Yearly Budget Worksheet** in Part Two where all your non-monthly expenses are listed on one convenient page.

Subscription Record

Publication:							

Subscription through:
   Agency
   Address							

Telephone							
Date Ordered							
Amount Paid							
Check # or Credit Card Used							
Length (1-2-3 yr.)							
Expiration Date							
Arrival Date							
Gift for:							
Other							

Mail Order Purchase Record

SHOPPING BY MAIL

Most mail or telephone purchases are through advertisements found in catalogs, brochures, newspapers, and magazines, as well as on TV and radio. There are advantages to shopping by mail, including convenience and saving time. However, how many times have you ordered something by mail or telephone (trusting it would arrive in 30 to 60 days), and it never arrived? Chances are, you've had your share of mail order frustrations and undelivered orders (which you may have even forgotten) and now recognize the value of keeping records for follow-up action.

HOW TO KEEP RECORDS

If orders do not arrive as scheduled and follow-up work is necessary, this Mail Order Purchase Record will be a valuable time- and money-saver for you.

Use this chart for all items ordered even if they are free. Log necessary information related to any purchases

Mail Order Purchase Record

Date Ordered					

Item(s) Ordered
    Title,
    Description,
    Number,
    Quantity,
    Color					

Source (Magazine, TV, Catalog)					

Company Name
    Telephone Number
    Address					

Price					
Total Sent					
How Paid (Credit card, Check number, Money order, C.O.D.)					
Date Received					
Follow-Up Notes (Date called/wrote, Contact person, Action taken)					

made by mail or telephone. When you happen to remember an item you ordered some time ago and realize it still has not arrived, you can go back to your records, see when you ordered the item, then follow up by telephone or mail, if necessary.

In some cases, it may be easier to cut out the advertisement with all the information given and tape it to the page, then fill in the "Total Sent" and "How Paid" sections. If you order a list of items from a catalog, make a copy of the order form and save it. On the chart, make a note of the order, the catalog date and how you paid for it.

When placing a telephone order, be especially careful to record all the information on the chart, including the name of the person who took your order.

FEDERAL TRADE COMMISSION (FTC) MAIL ORDER RULE

The Mail Order Rule of the Federal Trade Commission (FTC) requires companies to ship an order within the time period mentioned in their advertisements. If no time period is mentioned, the company is required to ship an order within 30 days of receipt of your payment. The company must notify you if it cannot make the shipment within 30 days and send you an option notice of either consenting to a delay or canceling the order for a refund.

For a free brochure on the Mail Order Rule, write the Federal Trade Commission, Pennsylvania Avenue N.W. at 6th Street, Washington, DC 20580.

Mail Order Purchase Record

Date Ordered					
Item(s) Ordered Title, Description, Number, Quantity, Color					
Source (Magazine, TV, Catalog)					
Company Name Telephone Number Address					
Price					
Total Sent					
How Paid (Credit card, Check number, Money order, C.O.D.)					
Date Received					
Follow-Up Notes (Date called/wrote, Contact person, Action taken)					

Recommended Reading

The following books and other resources are included because of their total focus or special sections on *budgeting, credit, debt, spending, money attitudes,* and/or *recovery issues.* If you want more financial planning information, there are numerous excellent books with a full range and comprehensive coverage of all facets of personal finance available at your local book stores and library.

If managing money is new for you, these books offer a variety of ideas, approaches and information to help you get started. The following books can provide complementary information as you do the practical hands-on part with *The Budget Kit: Common Cent$ Money Management Workbook.*

Beating the Paycheck-to-Paycheck Blues, John Ventura (Dearborn Financial Publishing, 1996).

Bill Griffeth's 10 Steps to Financial Prosperity (Probus Publishing Co., 1994).

Born to Spend: How to Overcome Compulsive Spending, Gloria Arenson (TAB Books, 1992).

The Cheapskate Monthly Money Makeover, Mary Hunt (St. Martin's Paperbacks, 1995).

The Complete Idiot's Guide to Managing Your Money, Robert K. Heady and Christy Heady (Alpha Books, 1995).

Consumer Reports Money Saving Tips for Good Times and Bad, by Walter B. Leonard and the editors of Consumer Reports Books (Consumer Reports Books, 1992).

Creating Money: Keys to Abundance, by Sanaya Roman and Duane Packer (H. J. Kramer Inc., 1988).

Credit, Cash and Co-Dependency: The Money Connection, by Yvonne Kaye, PhD (Health Communications Inc., 1991).

Cure Your Money Ills: Improve Your Self-Esteem Through Personal Budgeting, by Michael R. Slavit (R&E Publishers, 1992).

Cut Your Bills in Half: Thousands of Tips To Save Thousands of Dollars, by the editors of Rodale Press (Rodale Press, 1993).

Downsize Your Debt: How to Take Control of Your Personal Finances, Andrew Feinberg (Penguin Books, 1993).

Get Rich Slow, by Tama McAleese (Career Press, 1990).

Getting Rich on Any Income: 81 Ways to Increase Your Wealth Even if You've Been in Debt, Jeff Gomez (Citadel Press Book, 1994).

The Guide to Personal Budgeting: How to Stretch Your Dollars through Wise Money Management, David Scott (Globe Pequot Press, 1995).

The Guide to Saving Money, David L. Scott (The Globe Pequot Press, 1996).

How To Get Out of Debt, Stay Out of Debt & Live Prosperously, by Jerrold Mundis (Bantam Books, 1988). Based on the proven principles and techniques of Debtors Anonymous.

How to Get What You Want in Life with the Money You Already Have, Carol Keeffe, (Little Brown and Company, 1995).

How To Stop Fighting about Money and Make Some, by Adriane G. Berg (Avon Books, 1989).

How To Survive Without a Salary: Learning How To Live the Conserver Lifestyle, by Charles Long (Firefly Books, 1992)

How To Turn Your Money Life Around: The Money Books for Women, by Ruth Hayden (Health Communications Inc., 1992).

Kiplinger's Make Your Money Grow, by Theodore J. Miller, editor of *Changing Times* magazine (Kiplinger Books, 1993).

The Lifetime Book of Money Management, Grace Weinstein (Visible Ink Press, 1993).

Making the Most of Your Money: Smart Ways To Create Wealth and Plan Your Finances in the '90s, by Jane Bryant Quinn (Simon & Schuster, 1991).

Me and My Money; Book One: Writing a Money Autobiography, by Karen McCall (Financial Recovery Press, 1990).

Money Advice for Your Successful Remarriage: Handling Delicate Financial Issues with Love and Understanding, Patricia Schiff Estess (Betterway Books, 1996).

The Money Diet: Reaping the Rewards of Financial Fitness, Ginger Applegarth (Penguin Books, 1995).

Money Doesn't Grow on Trees: A Parent's Guide to Raising Financially Responsible Children, Neale S. Godfrey and Carolina Edwards, (Simon and Schuster, 1994).

Money, How To Get It, Keep It, and Make It Grow, by Tama McAleese (Career Press, 1991).

Money for Life: The "Money Makeover" That Will End Your Worries and Secure Your Dreams, by Steve Crowley (Simon & Schuster, 1991).

Money Grows on Trees: How To Make, Manage and Master Money, by Alton Howard (Howard Publishers, 1991).

Money Love: How To Get the Money You Deserve for Whatever You Want, by Jerry Gilles (Warner Books, 1994).

Money Mastery In Just Minutes a Day, Fred E. Waddell (Dearborn Financial Publishing, 1996).

The New Money Workbook for Women: A Step by Step Guide To Managing Your Personal Finances, by Carole Phillips (Brick House Publishing Co., 1988).

Ninety Days to Financial Fitness, Joan German-Grapes (Collier Books, 1993).

1001 Ways To Cut Your Expenses, by Jonathan D. Pond (Dell Publishing, 1992).

Overcoming Overspending: A Winning Plan for Spenders and Their Partners, Olivia Mellan (Walker and Company, 1995).

Penny Pinching: How To Lower Your Everyday Expenses Without Lowering Your Standard of Living, by Lee and Barbara Simmons (Bantam Books, 1994).

Personal Finance for Dummies, Eric Tyson (IDG Books, 1996).

Prospering Woman: A Complete Guide To Achieving the Full Abundant Life, by Ruth Ross, PhD (Bantam Books, 1995).

Richest Man in Babylon, George S. Clason (Signet, 1995).

Terry Savage Talks Money: The Common-Sense Guide to Money Matters, by Terry Savage (Harper Collins, 1993).

The Smart Woman's Guide to Spending, Saving, and Managing Money, Diane Pearl and Ellie Williams Clinton (Career Press, 1994)

10 Minute Guide to Beating Debt, Susan Abentrod (Macmillan Spectrum/Alpha, 1996).

Turn Chaos into Cash: The Complete Guide To Organizing and Managing Your Personal Finances, by Jean Ross Peterson (Betterway Publications, Inc., 1989).

The Ultimate Credit Handbook: How to Double Your Credit, Cut Your Debt, and Have a Lifetime of Great Credit, Gerri Detweiler (Plume, 1993).

The Way to Save—A 10-Step Blueprint for Lifetime Security, by Ginita Wall (Henry Holt and Company, 1993).

Wealth Without Risk, by Charles Givens (Simon & Schuster, 1988).

Women and Money: A Guide for the 90s, by Anita Jones-Lee (Barron's, 1991).

You're Not Overdrawn—Just Underdeposited, or How to Live with Class on Little Money, Beverlee Kelley (Griffin Publishing, 1992).

Your Financial Guide: Advice for Every Stage of Your Life, Ray Martin (Macmillan Spectrum, 1996).

Your Personal Financial Fitness Program: A Step by Step Guide to Managing Your Money, Elizabeth S. Lewin (Facts on File, 1995).

Your Wealth-Building Years, by Adriane G. Berg (Newmarket Press, 1994).

Other Resources

National Center for Financial Education, The Money-Book Store Catalog, P.O. Box 34070, San Diego, CA 92163-4070 (Great comprehensive listing of good basic money books including books about children and money and books especially for women.)

Bankcard Holders of America, 524 Branch Dr., Salem, VA 24153—a national nonprofit credit education advocacy group. Membership is $24 and includes the bimonthly newsletter, *Bankcard Consumer News,* and credit education publications dealing with money management, credit rights, and debt reduction.

The Pocket Change Investor, Good Advice Press, Box 78, Elizaville, NY 12523, $12.95/yr.—A quarterly newsletter packed with information to help you save money on your debt, cut expenses, and live better on less.

Index

About the Author

Judy Lawrence, MS Ed., is a financial counselor and popular speaker on basic money management. She has been a featured guest on numerous television and radio shows throughout the country. *The Budget Kit* was originally developed while she was a college counselor counseling reentry widowed and divorced women students with limited budgeting experience. It soon became apparent that budgeting and saving issues were a universal concern to all populations. Judy saw the need for a nonintimidating workbook that could immediately be used by people with limited time or limited organizing and budgeting skills. In addition to her own private consulting firm in Albuquerque, New Mexico, where she counsels couples, individuals, and small businesses, Ms. Lawrence is a court-appointed expert who develops and evaluates personal budgets in divorce cases. Her techniques and workbooks, including *The Money Tracker* and *The Family Memory Book,* are basic, encouraging, and extremely user-friendly.

To arrange for speaking engagements or telephone consultations with Judy Lawrence, call 505-296-8792 or e-mail jlawrence@thuntek.net. You can also visit her web site at http://www.thuntek.net/~jlmoney.